PENGUIN B

Suffragette

Barbara Bodichon

Frances Power Cobbe

Christabel Pankhurst

Emmeline Pankhurst

Annie Kenney

Flora Drummond

Eva Gore-Booth

Constance Smedley

Margaret McMillan

Maud Arncliffe Sennett

Selina Cooper

Sophia Duleep Singh

Sylvia Pankhurst

Emily Wilding Davison

Millicent Garrett Fawcett

Suffragette Manifestos

PENGUIN BOOKS — GREAT IDEAS

PENGUIN BOOKS

UK | USA | Canada | Ireland | Australia
India | New Zealand | South Africa

Penguin Books is part of the Penguin Random House group
of companies whose addresses can be found at
global.penguinrandomhouse.com.

This selection published in Penguin Books 2020
001

The material here has been sourced from newspaper articles,
books, pamphlets, posters and legal documents published between
1869 and 1920

Sylvia Pankhurst's 'The Woman's Dreadnought' reproduced
with the permission of the Pankhurst family.

'Speeches by members of the Women's Social and Political Union'
reproduced with the permission of the Pankhurst family and the
Kenney family, and with thanks to The Women's Library, LSE Library.

'Extract from Special Branch Report' reproduced with the
permission of the Kenney family.

Set in 11.2/13.75 pt Dante MT Std
Typeset by Jouve (UK), Milton Keynes
Printed and bound in Great Britain by Clays Ltd, Elcograf S.p.A.

A CIP catalogue record for this book is available from the British Library

ISBN: 978-0-241-47241-5

www.greenpenguin.co.uk

Penguin Random House is committed to a
sustainable future for our business, our readers
and our planet. This book is made from Forest
Stewardship Council® certified paper.

Contents

Contents

Fourteen Reasons for Supporting Women's Suffrage

1. – Because it is the foundation of all political liberty that those who obey the Law should be able to have a voice in choosing those who make the Law.
2. – Because Parliament should be the reflection of the wishes of the people.
3. – Because Parliament cannot fully reflect the wishes of the people, when the wishes of women are without any direct representation.
4. – Because most Laws affect women as much as men, and some Laws affect women especially.
5. – Because the Laws which affect women especially are now passed without consulting those persons whom they are intended to benefit.
6. – Because Laws affecting children should be regarded from the woman's point of view as well as the man's.
7. – Because every session questions affecting the home come up for consideration in Parliament.
8. – Because women have experience which should be helpfully brought to bear on domestic legislation.
9. – Because to deprive women of the vote is to lower their position in common estimation.

10. – Because the possession of the vote would increase the sense of responsibility amongst women towards questions of public importance.
11. – Because public-spirited mothers make public-spirited sons.
12. – Because large numbers of intelligent, thoughtful, hard-working women desire the franchise.
13. – Because the objections raised against their having the franchise are based on sentiment, not on reason.
14. – Because – to sum all reasons up in one – it is for the common good of all.

The National Union of Women's
Suffragette Societies

Reasons for and against the Enfranchisement of Women

BARBARA BODICHON

That a respectable, orderly, independent body in the State should have no voice, and no influence recognised by the law, in the election of the representatives of the people, while they are otherwise acknowledged as responsible citizens, are eligible for many public offices, and required to pay all taxes, is an anomaly which seems to require some explanation. Many people are unable to conceive that women can care about voting. That some women do care, has been proved by the Petitions presented to Parliament. I shall try to show why some care – and why those who do not, ought to be made to care.

There are now a very considerable number of open-minded, unprejudiced people, who see no particular reason why women should not have votes, if they want them; but, they ask, what would be the good of it? What is there that women want which male legislators are not willing to give? And here let me say at the outset, that the advocates of this measure are very far from accusing men of deliberate unfairness to women. It is not as a means of extorting justice from unwilling legislators that the franchise is claimed for women. In so far as the claim is made with any special reference to class interests at all, it is simply on the general ground that under a representative government, any class which is not represented is likely to be neglected. Proverbially, what is out of sight is out of mind; and the theory that women, as such, are bound to keep out of sight, finds its most emphatic expression in the denial of the right to vote. The direct results are probably less injurious than those which are indirect; but that a want of due consideration for the interests of women is apparent in our legislation, could very easily be shown. To give evidence in detail would be a long and an invidious task. I will mention one instance only, that of the educational endowments all over the country. Very few people would now maintain that the education of boys is more important to the State than that of girls. But as a matter of fact, girls have but a very small share in educational endowments. Many of the old foundations have been reformed by Parliament, but the desirableness of providing with equal care for girls and boys has very seldom been recognised. In the administration of charities generally, the same tendency prevails to postpone the claims of women to those of men.

Among instances of hardship traceable directly to exclusion from the franchise and to no other cause, may be mentioned the unwillingness of landlords to accept women as tenants. Two large farmers in Suffolk inform me that this is not an uncommon case. They mention one estate on which seven widows have been ejected, who, if they had had votes, would have been continued as tenants.

The case of women farmers is stronger, but not much stronger, than that of women who, as heads of a business or a household, fulfil the duties of a man in the same position. Their task is often a hard one, and everything which helps to sustain their self-respect, and to give them consideration and importance in the eyes of others, is likely to lessen their difficulties and make them happier and stronger for the battle of life. The very fact that, though householders and taxpayers, they have not equal privileges with male householders and taxpayers, is in itself a *deconsideration*, which seems to me invidious and useless. It casts a kind of slur on the value of their opinions; and I may remark in passing, that what is treated as of no value is apt to grow valueless. Citizenship is an honour, and not to have the full rights of a citizen is a want of honour. Obvious it may not be, but by a subtle and sure process, those who without their own consent and without sufficient reason are debarred from full participation in the rights and duties of a citizen, lose more or less of social consideration and esteem.

These arguments, founded on considerations of justice and mercy to a large and important and increasing class, might in a civilised country, and in the absence of strong reasons to the contrary, be deemed amply sufficient to justify the measure proposed. There remain to be considered those aspects of the question which affect the general community. And among all the reasons for giving women votes, the one which appears to me the strongest, is that of the influence it might be expected to have in increasing public spirit. Patriotism, a healthy, lively, intelligent interest in everything which concerns the nation to which we belong, and an unselfish devotedness to the public service, – these are the qualities which make a people great and happy; these are the virtues which ought to be most sedulously cultivated in all classes of the community. And I know no better means, at this present time, of counteracting the tendency to prefer narrow private ends to the public good, than this of giving to all women, duly qualified, a direct and conscious participation in political affairs. Give some women votes, and it will tend to make all women think seriously of the concerns of the nation at large, and their interest having once been fairly roused, they will take pains, by reading and by consultation with persons better informed than themselves, to form sound opinions. As it is, women of the middle class occupy themselves but little with anything beyond their own family circle. They do not consider it any concern of theirs, if poor men and women are ill-nursed in work-house infirmaries, and poor children ill-taught in workhouse schools. If the roads are bad, the drains neglected, the water poisoned, they think it is all very wrong, but it does not occur to them that it is their duty to get it put right. These farmer-women and business-women have honest, sensible minds and much practical experience, but they do not bring their good sense to bear upon public affairs, because they think it is men's business, not theirs, to look after such things. It is this belief – so narrowing and deadening in its influence – that the exercise of the franchise would tend to dissipate. The mere fact of being called upon to enforce an opinion by a vote, would have an immediate effect in awakening a healthy sense of responsibility. There is no reason why these women should not take an active interest in all the social questions – education, public health, prison discipline, the poor laws, and the rest – which occupy Parliament, and they would be much more likely to do so, if they felt that they had importance in the eyes of members of Parliament, and could claim a hearing for their opinions.

Besides these women of business, there are ladies of property, whose more active participation in public affairs would be beneficial both to themselves and the community generally. The want of stimulus to energetic action is much felt by women of the higher classes. It is agreed that they ought not to be idle, but what they ought to do is not so clear. Reading, music and drawing, needlework, and charity are their usual employments. Reading, without a purpose, does not come to much. Music and drawing, and needlework, are most commonly regarded as amusements intended to fill up time. We have left, as the serious duty of independent and unmarried women, the care of the poor in all its branches, including visiting the sick and the aged, and ministering to their wants, looking after the schools, and in every possible way giving help wherever help is needed. Now education, the relief of the destitute, and the health of the people, are among the most important and difficult matters which occupy the minds of statesmen, and if it is admitted that women of leisure and culture are bound to contribute their part towards the solution of these great questions, it is evident that every means of making their co-operation enlightened and vigorous should be sought for. They have special opportunities of observing the operation of many of the laws. They know, for example, for they see before their eyes, the practical working of the law of settlement – of the laws relating to the dwellings of the poor – and many others, and the experience which peculiarly qualifies them to form a judgment on these matters ought not to be thrown away. We all know that we have already a goodly body of rich, influential working-women, whose opinions on the social and political questions of the day are well worth listening to. In almost every parish there are, happily for England, such women. Now everything should be done to give these valuable members of the community a solid social standing. If they are wanted – and there can be no doubt that they are – in all departments of social work, their position in the work should be as dignified and honourable as it is possible to make it. Rich unmarried women have many opportunities of benefiting the community, which are not within reach of a married woman, absorbed by the care of her husband and children. Everything, I say again, should be done to encourage this most important and increasing class to take their place in the army of workers for the common good, and all the forces we can bring to bear for this end are of incalculable value. For by bringing women into hearty co-operation with men, we gain the benefit not only of their work, but of their intelligent sympathy. Public spirit is like fire: a feeble spark of it may be fanned into a flame, or it may very easily be put out. And the result of teaching women that they have nothing to do with politics, is that their influence goes towards extinguishing the unselfish interest – never too strong – which men are disposed to take in public affairs.

Let each member of the House of Commons consider, in a spirit of true scientific enquiry, all the properly qualified women of his acquaintance, and he will see no reason why the single ladies and the widows among his own family and friends should not form as sensible opinions on the merits of candidates as the voters who returned him to Parliament. When we find among the disfranchised such names as those of Mrs Somerville, Harriet Martineau, Miss Burdett Coutts, Florence Nightingale, Mary Carpenter, Louisa Twining, Miss Marsh, and many others scarcely inferior to these in intellectual and moral worth, we cannot but desire, for the elevation and dignity of the parliamentary system, to add them to the number of electors.

It need scarcely be pointed out that the measure has nothing of a party character. We have precedents under two very different governments, those of Austria and Sweden, for something very similar to what is now proposed. Now, let us calmly consider all the arguments we have heard against giving the franchise to women.

Among these, the first and commonest is – Women do not want votes. Certainly that is a capital reason why women should not have votes thrust upon them, and no one proposes compulsory registration. There are many men who do not care to use their votes, and there is no law compelling them either to register themselves or to vote. The statement, however, that women do not wish to vote, is a mere assertion, and may be met by a counter-assertion. Some women do want votes, which the petitions signed, and now in course of signature, go very largely to prove. Some women manifestly do; others, let it be admitted, do not. It is impossible to say positively which side has the majority, unless we could poll all the women in question; or, in other words, without resorting to the very measure which is under discussion. Make registration possible, and we shall see how many care to avail themselves of the privilege.

But, it is said, women have other duties. The function of women is different to that of men, and their function is not politics. It is very true that women have other duties – many and various. But so have men. No citizen lives for his citizen duties only. He is a professional man, a tradesman, a family man, a club man, a thousand things as well as a voter. Of course these occupations sometimes interfere with a man's duties as a citizen, and when he cannot vote, he cannot. So with women; when they cannot vote, they cannot.

The proposition we are discussing, practically concerns only single women and widows who have 40s. freeholds, or other county qualifications, and for boroughs, all those who occupy, as owners or tenants, houses of the value of £10 a year. Among these there are surely a great number whose time is not fully occupied, not even so much as that of men. Their duties in sickrooms and in caring for children, leave them a sufficient margin of leisure for reading newspapers, and studying the *pros* and *cons* of political and social questions. No one can mean seriously to affirm that widows and unmarried women would find the mere act of voting once in several years arduous. One day, say once in three years, might surely be spared from domestic duties. If it is urged that it is not the time spent in voting that is in question, but the thought and the attention which are necessary for forming political opinions, I reply that women of the class we are speaking of, have, as a rule, more time for thought than men, their duties being of a less engrossing character, and they ought to bestow a considerable amount of thought and attention on the questions which occupy the Legislature. Social matters occupy every day a larger space in the deliberations of Parliament, and on many of these questions women are led to think and to judge in the fulfilment of those duties which, as a matter of course, devolve upon them in the ordinary business of English life. And however important the duties of home may be, we must bear in mind that a woman's duties do not end there. She is a daughter, a sister, the mistress of a household; she ought to be, in the broadest sense of the word, a neighbour, both to her equals and to the poor. These are her obvious and undeniable duties, and within the limits of her admitted functions; I should think it desirable to add to them – duties to her parish and to the State. A woman who is valuable in all the relations of life, a woman of a large nature, will be more perfect in her domestic capacity, and not less.

If we contemplate women in the past, and in different countries, we find them acting, in addition to their domestic part, all sorts of different *rôles*. What was their *rôle* among the Jews and the Romans? What was it in the early Christian churches? What is it amongst the Quakers? What is it in the colliery districts, – at the court of Victoria, and the Tuileries? We can conjure up thousands of pictures of women performing different functions under varying conditions. They have done and do, all sorts of work in all sorts of ways. Is there anything in the past history of the world, which justifies the assertion that they must and will do certain things in the future, and will not and cannot do certain other things? I do not think there is.

But to return to my argument, and supposing that there were enough data in the past to enable us to predict that women will never take sufficient interest in politics to induce even widows and single women to wish to vote once in several years, should we be justified in realising our own prediction, and forbidding by law what we declare to be contrary to nature? If anyone believes, as the result of observation and experience, that it is not a womanly function to vote, I respect such belief, and answer – only the future can prove. But what I do not respect, is the strange want of toleration which says – 'You shall not do this or that.' We do not want to compel women to act; we only wish to see them free to exercise or not, according as they themselves desire, political and other functions.

The argument that 'women are ignorant of politics,' would have great force if it could be shown that the mass of the existing voters are thoroughly well informed on political subjects, or even much better informed than the persons to whom it is proposed to give votes. Granted that women are ignorant of politics, so are many male ten-pound householders. Their ideas are not always clear on political questions, and would probably be even more confused if they had not votes. No mass of human beings will or can undertake the task of form-ing opinions on matters over which they have no control, and on which they have no practical decision to make. It would by most persons be considered a waste of time. When women have votes, they will read with closer attention than heretofore the daily histories of our times, and will converse with each other and with their fathers and brothers about social and political questions. They will become interested in a wider circle of ideas, and where they now think and feel somewhat vaguely, they will form definite and decided opinions.

Among the women who are disqualified for voting by the legal disability of sex, there is a large number of the educated class. We shall know the exact number of women possessing the household and property qualifi-cations, when the return ordered by Parliament has been made. In the meantime, the following calculation is suggestive. In the 'London Court Guide,' which of course includes no houses below the value of £10 a year, the number of householders whose names begin with A is 1149. Of these, 205, that is more than one-sixth, are women, all of whom are either unmarried or widows.

The fear entertained by some persons that family dissension would result from encouraging women to form political opinions, might be urged with equal force against their having any opinions on any subject at all. Differences on religious subjects are still more apt to rouse the passions and create disunion than political differences. As for opinions causing disunion, let it be remembered that what is a possible cause of disunion is also a possible cause of deeply-founded union. The more rational women become, the more real union there will be in families, for nothing separates so much as unreasonableness and frivolity. It will be said, perhaps, that contrary opinions may be held by the different members of a family without bringing on quarrels, so long as they are kept to the region of theory, and no attempt is made to carry them out publicly in action. But religious differences must be shown publicly. A woman who determines upon changing her religion – say to go over from Protestantism to Romanism – proclaims her difference from her family in a public and often a very distressing manner. But no one has yet proposed to make it illegal for a woman to change her religion. After all – is it essential that brothers and sisters and cousins shall all vote on the same side?

An assertion often made, that women would lose the

good influence which they now exert indirectly on public affairs if they had votes, seems to require proof. First
of all, it is necessary to prove that women have this indirect influence, – then that it is good, – then that the
indirect good influence would be lost if they had direct
influence, – then that the indirect influence which they
would lose is better than the direct influence they would
gain. From my own observation I should say, that the
women who have gained by their wisdom and earnest-
ness a good indirect influence, would not lose that
influence if they had votes. And I see no necessary con-
nexion between goodness and indirectness. On the
contrary, I believe that the great thing women want is
to be more direct and straightforward in thought, word,
and deed. I think the educational advantage of citizenship to women would be so great, that I feel inclined to
run the risk of sacrificing the subtle indirect influence,
to a wholesome feeling of responsibility, which would,
I think, make women give their opinions less rashly
and more conscientiously than at present on political
subjects.

A gentleman who thinks much about details, affirms
that 'polling-booths are not fit places for women.' If this
is so, one can only say that the sooner they are made fit
the better. That in a State which professes to be civilised, a solemn public duty can only be discharged in the
midst of drunkenness and riot, is scandalous and not to
be endured. It is no doubt true, that in many places polling is now carried on in a turbulent and disorderly
manner. Where that is unhappily the case, women

clearly must stay away. Englishwomen can surely be trusted not to force their way to the polling-booth when it would be manifestly unfit. But it does not follow that, because in some disreputable places some women would be illegally, but with their own consent, prevented from recording their votes, therefore all women, in all places, should be, without their own consent, by law disqualified. Those who at the last election visited the polling places in London and Westminster, and many other places, will bear me out in asserting, that a lady would have had no more difficulty or annoyance to encounter in giving her vote, than she has in going to the Botanical Gardens or to Westminster Abbey.

There are certain other difficulties sometimes vaguely brought forward by the unreflecting, which I shall not attempt to discuss. Such, for example, is the argument that as voters ought to be independent, and as married women are liable to be influenced by their husbands, therefore unmarried women and widows ought not to vote. Or again, that many ladies canvass, and canvassing by ladies is a very objectionable practice, therefore canvassing ought to be the only direct method by which women can bring their influence to bear upon an election. Into such objections it is not necessary here to enter.

Nor is it needful to discuss the extreme logical consequences which may be obtained by pressing to an undue length the arguments used in favour of permitting women to exercise the suffrage. The question under consideration is, not whether women ought logically to be members of Parliament, but whether, under existing circumstances, it is for the good of the State that women, who perform most of the duties, and enjoy nearly all the rights of citizenship, should be by special enactment disabled from exercising the additional privilege of taking part in the election of the representatives of the people. It is a question of expediency, to be discussed calmly, without passion or prejudice.

In England, the extension proposed would interfere with no vested interests. It would involve no change in the principles on which our Government is based, but would rather make our Constitution more consistent with itself. Conservatives have a right to claim it as a Conservative measure. Liberals are bound to ask for it as a necessary part of radical reform. There is no reason for identifying it with any class or party in the State, and it is, in fact, impossible to predict what influence it might have on party politics. The question is simply of a special legal disability, which must, sooner or later, be removed.

Our Policy: An Address to Women concerning the Suffrage

FRANCES POWER COBBE

There is an instructive story, told by Herodotus, of an African nation which went to war with the South Wind. The wind had greatly annoyed these Psyllians by drying up their cisterns, so they organized a campaign and set off to attack the enemy at head-quarters – somewhere, I presume, about the Sahara. The army was admirably equipped with all the military engines of those days – swords and spears, darts and javelins, battering rams and catapults. It happened that the South Wind did not, however, suffer much from these weapons, but got up one fine morning and blew! – The sands of the desert have lain for a great many ages over those unfortunate Psyllians; and, as Herodotus placidly concludes the story, 'The Nasamones possess the territory of those who thus perished.'

It seems to me that we women who have been fighting for the Suffrage with logical arguments – syllogisms, analogies, demonstrations, and reductions-to-the-absurd of our antagonists' position, in short, all the weapons of ratiocinative warfare – have been behaving very much like those poor Psyllians, who imagined that darts, and swords, and catapults would avail against the Simoon. The obvious truth is, that it is Sentiment we have to contend against, not Reason; Feeling and Pre-possession, not intellectual Conviction. Had Logic been the only obstacle in our way, we should long ago have been polling our votes for Parliamentary as well as for Municipal and School Board elections. To those who hold that Property is the thing intended to be repre-sented by the Constitution of England, we have shown that we possess such property. To those who say that Tax-paying and Representation should go together, we have pointed to the tax-gatherers' papers, which, alas! lie on our hall-tables wholly irrespective of the touch-ing fact that we belong to the 'protected sex.' Where Intelligence, Education, and freedom from crime are considered enough to confer rights of citizenship, we have remarked that we are quite ready to challenge rivalry in such particulars with those Illiterates for whose exercise of political functions our Senate has taken such exemplary care. Finally, to the ever-recurring charge that we cannot fight, and therefore ought not to vote, we have replied that the logic of the exclusion will be manifest when all the men too weak, too short, or too old for the military standard be likewise disfran-chised, and when the actual soldiers of our army are accorded the suffrage.

But, as I began by remarking, it is Sentiment, not Logic, against which we have to struggle; and we shall best do so, I think, by endeavouring to understand and make full allowance for it; and then by steadily working shoulder to shoulder so as to conquer, or rather *win* it over to our side. There is nothing astonishing or blameworthy in the fact that both men and women (women even more than men), when they first hear of the proposal that political action should be shared by both sexes, are startled and shocked. The wonder would be if, after witnessing women's inaction for thousands of years, the set of our brains were *not* to see them for ever 'suckling fools and chronicling small-beer.' The 'hereditary transmission of psychical habits,' which Dr Carpenter talks of, could not fail to leave such an impression; nay, a very short period of seclusion would have sufficed to stamp a prejudice against our ever taking part in public affairs. I had myself the misfortune at one time to consult fourteen eminent surgeons concerning a sprained ankle, and, as a result of that gross imprudence, to pass four of the best years of life as a miserable cripple upon crutches. At the end of that period, when my friends saw me once more walking erect and free, they unanimously exclaimed, 'Oh, do not attempt it! For pity's sake do not go into the street!' One of the tenderest of them even added, almost in tears, 'I cannot *endure* to see you going about without your crutches!' Of course I had much difficulty in persuading these kind people that there was really nothing indecent, or even unladylike, in making use of the limbs wherewith nature had provided me. But I succeeded at last; and so I think women in general will eventually succeed in converting the world to the notion that the faculties bestowed on us by Providence – whether they be great or small – ought all to be used. Humanity might very properly be represented by a man who has all his life used his right hand vigorously, but has kept his left in a sling. Whether the limb were originally weaker than the right, and could not have done as good work, it is not easy to say. It is quite certainly now a poor sinister arm, soft, tender, and without muscular force, and so long accustomed to hang from the neck, that when by chance it is set to work it begins to move in a very nervous and unpractised fashion. Nevertheless, unless any one be prepared to maintain that a man is the better for keeping his left hand tied up, and doing his work with his right alone, it must, I think, be obvious, that this same Humanity will be considerably more happy, and perform its labour more satisfactorily, with two free arms than one.

To win over the public Sentiment now opposed to it, to this great and portentous emancipation of the Left Hand from its sling, very many different sagacious methods will, I am sure, suggest themselves to my readers. I shall venture merely to offer a few hints, which appear to me most important, regarding, 1st, the things which we women ought to *stop doing* and *being*, and, 2ndly, the things we ought to begin to *do* and to *be*.

For the first, we decidedly ought (if we can) to cease to be silly. It is very tempting, I understand, to be silly, when silliness is obviously infinitely more attractive than sense, and when a sweet little piece of utter folly is received as 'so charming' by all who are privileged to hear it. The lady who said (or perhaps did not say) to one of our eminent senators, that 'if she had a vote she would sell it directly to the candidate who would give her a pair of diamond ear-rings' – that sweet young thing (if she ever had existence) was no doubt rewarded by the cordial and gallant approbation of the representative of the masculine gender to whom she confided her elevated views. Nevertheless, her silly speech, and the tens of thousands of speeches in the same vein, made in every ball-room in the kingdom, serve, like so many flakes of snow, to hide the ground. The woman who makes one of them with an ingenious simper, generally has her reward in a rapturous smile; but she has done in that moment of folly all that lay in her power to defer a measure of justice on which hangs, more or less directly, the moral and physical welfare of thousands of women.

Nor is it only, or chiefly, by directly scoffing at the demand for Woman Suffrage that silly women hurt our cause. They hurt us much more by showing themselves unfit for it; by perpetuating the delusion that women are so many kittens – charming to play with, but no more fit to be given political rights than Caligula's horse to be made a Consul. In looking over an American journal devoted to our interests, I have just fallen on three names in succession, which alone seem (very unjustly no doubt) to place the ladies who are willing to bear them through this serious mortal life, rather in the kittenish than the womanly category. Think of gravely demanding political influence, and then signing oneself as Miss 'Mettie' Wauchop, Miss 'Lulu' Wilkinson, or Miss 'Vinnie' Ream! Silly Dress is a subject so portentous, and on which I feel so little competent to speak, that I shall only remark that, while true taste in attire must always add a pleasant prepossession in favour of everything a woman may ask of right or respect, the style which betrays that hours have been devoted to devising it, is absolutely prohibitive of such consideration. The human soul which has been occupied for an entire morning, like one of Pope's sprites, striving –

> 'Invention to bestow,
> To change a flounce, or add a furbelow,'

has, by the hypothesis, neither leisure nor inclination for the graver and nobler pursuits of a rational being.

Another point on which it behoves us women to mend our ways, is the matter of Courage. Men give courage the first place among the virtues, because, without it, there is no guarantee for any other virtue. Assuredly this principle applies no less to women, who, if they be cowards, may be bullied or coerced into every kind of falsehood and baseness, like Ingoldsby's Duchess of Cleves, when her husband pinched her to make her betray her friends –

> 'His hard iron gauntlet, the flesh went an inch in,
> She didn't mind death, but she couldn't stand
>   pinching.'

If we cannot 'stand pinching,' in more ways than one, slaves we are and slaves we must ever be, whether civil and political rights are given to us or not. When I hear a woman say, with a complacent smile, as if she were announcing an ornament of her reputation, 'O, I am *such* a coward!' I always feel inclined to say, 'Indeed? And, may I ask, do you ever go about boasting – "O, I am such a liar?" If you are really a coward you will become a liar any day.' Because we have more sensitive nervous systems than men is no reason why honour, and conscience, and self-respect should not teach us to dominate them. I have no doubt there are some virtues, like Temperance, which cost a man more self-control to exercise than they cost a woman, but we do not hold him exonerated on that account if he fail to exert such self-government. We may pity a woman who cannot stop herself from shrieking if a horse runs away, or a boat tosses on the waves; but assuredly we do not feel she is a person to be trusted with an important charge. On the other hand, the sight of a weak, and perhaps sickly or aged woman, calm, silent, and resolute in the face of peril, is a thing never to be forgotten; and the veriest jackanapes alive who expresses his sublime horror of a 'strong-minded female' will bless his good fortune that it is in her carriage or boat he is sitting, and not in that of the shrieking Angelina.

There are many more things which we ought to refrain from doing if we desire to conquer public Senti-ment to our side; but I must hasten to the second part of my subject – the things which we Ought to Do for that end. In the first place, we ought to perform our present share in the world's work – the housekeeping, the house-adorning, the child-educating – so as to prove that, before we go a step further, we can and will at least do *this*. Before Political Economy comes the Economy of the Kitchen, the Larder, and the Coal-cellar; and before the national Budget the household weekly bills. I do not say that the wife, daughter, and sister who manages a house with perfect order and frugality, to the comfort of all the in-dwellers, will thereby convince them of her right to the Suffrage; but I am quite sure, that if she neglect so to manage the house, or live in a despicable muddle of eternal strife with her servants, she will very completely prove her *un*fitness for any higher functions.

Next, we should, as much as possible, seek for employments of the kind for which we are suited, but which have been hitherto monopolized by men; and when we have chanced to obtain one, we should take good care not to lose it by fitful, irregular attendance, slovenly work, or any appeal whatever to special consideration *as women*. Secretaryships, clerkships, telegraph and post-office work, and especially work on the public press (wherein our influence can be direct, as well as indirect), are all objects of concern. I rejoiced much recently to see thirty charming young ladies, the daughters of professional men, at work in the Prudential Insurance Office on Ludgate Hill; and as many more painting porcelain for Messrs Minton at South Kensington. Mr Stansfeld's generous appointment of Mrs Nassau Senior, to report to Government on the condition of pauper girls in London, and that lady's admirable performance of her task, will, I trust, lead ere long to the regular employment, by the State, of Female Inspectors of workhouses, schools, and asylums of all kinds wherein either women or children find refuge. I do not hesitate to say that one woman who does such work as this – even the humblest of those I have named – steadily and thoroughly, does at the same time more for the cause of Woman Suffrage than one who clamours for it most vehemently, but does nothing to prove the fitness of her sex for any public function.

Lastly, we must avail ourselves with the utmost care and conscientiousness of every fragment of Civil Rights which have hitherto been conceded to us. Not the election of a Poor Law Guardian or a parish Churchwarden, still less a municipal election, ought to pass without all the female ratepayers giving their votes, and showing that they do so intelligently, and after due enquiry. If it were possible for us to act in each locality mainly in concert – a committee of the more leisurely obtaining and transmitting the information needed – and everywhere upholding the best candidates, our action would in time come to be felt throughout the country. As to the School Board elections, had they been devised expressly as a prelude and preparation for women's entrance into political life, we could not have had anything better, and we must needs regret that, as yet, they have been very inadequately utilized for such purpose. The ladies who have fought the good fight, and their generous male supporters, deserve from us the heartiest thanks, whether they have or have not proved successful.

The sentiments of men about women must necessarily be formed on the characters of those with whom they associate. If a man's mother be a fool, and his sisters 'Girls of the Period,' and if he select for himself the society of ladies of the *demi-monde*, or of that section of the *grand monde* which emulates the *demi-monde* as closely as it dares, it is quite obvious that when the abstract idea 'Woman' is suggested to him, he will think of a creature in paint, powder, and chignon, whose breath of life is the admiration of men like himself, and who has no more heart, mind, or conscience than a broomstick. He will tell you, and tell you truly, that a woman – such as he knows the creature – loves nobody in earnest, but is ready to pretend to love anybody who will marry her and make her rich; that she is envious of all her female friends, especially the pretty ones; and that she has neither fixed religious nor political opinions, but only pretends ardently to adopt those which she thinks will commend her to the man whom she desires to attract. When I hear a man talk in a mode which implies that this is, at bottom, his idea of a woman, I always make a private memorandum regarding the quarter whence he must have derived his models; just as when I was an *habitué* of the Roman studios I knew precisely from which old beggarman on the steps of the *Trinità* one painter had taken his 'Jupiter,' and from which damsel of uncertain morals another had copied his 'Madonna

Immacolata.' Of course I am not afterwards surprised when such a man answers the demand for Woman Suffrage by such laughs as resound through the House of Commons when the subject is broached.

> 'Who would care for a doll, though its ringlets
> were curled
> And its petticoats cut in the fashion?'

If women *be* dolls, none but children would play the farce of giving them political rights – in a Baby-house State. The only question is, *Are* they toys? Or is the opinion of the men who find (or make) them so, the one to be acted upon?

On the other hand, if a man's mother be a wise and loving woman, if his sisters be innocent-hearted and intelligent girls, and if he have associated in manhood from preference with good and sensible women, the notion which he forms of the other sex is absolutely the reverse of all I have described. He knows that a woman is capable of love – motherly, conjugal, sisterly – the purest, most disinterested, and most tender. He knows that, so far from being without fixed opinions, she is apt to hold those which she has early acquired with too rigid and narrow a prejudice; and that the ideas of duty and religion occupy commonly a far larger space in her mind than in those of the majority of his male companions. Lastly, by one curious test, his view of woman may always be discriminated from that of the man who has preferred to associate with the *Hetaira* order of female. He will know that, instead of being jealous of her associates, the true woman generally carries her loving admiration for the gifts and graces of her female friends to the verge of exaggeration, and glories in their achievements in educational competitions, in literature, and art, with a generous enthusiasm not often found among masculine rivals. He will take, for example, the letters published in Mrs Somerville's 'Recollections,' which passed between that lady and Mrs Marcet, Miss Edgworth, Miss Berry, and Mrs Joanna Baillie – each expressing her warm delight in the other's gifts and successes – as precisely the most natural outcome of the feelings of women of their class for one another.

To a man trained to think thus of women, the proposal that they should begin to take a part in public affairs, may indeed, at first, seem startling, even offensive; but it will be because he has thought so highly of them, not so lowly. By degrees, perhaps, he will come to learn that the Niche does not make a Saint, and that Idleness is not the root of all good for women, while it is that of all evil for men. Possibly, at last, he will think as the devout Dr Upham said at the close of his life – that, 'since the coming of Christ, no event has promised so much for the virtue and happiness of the human race as the admission of Woman into a share of public duty.'

Thus then, it seems clear, that if the Sentiment of men is to be won over to the claims of women, it must be by compelling them to recognize as the true ideal of womanhood, not a Phryne or a Ninon, but a Zenobia or a Madame Roland.

The great obstacle to the concession of the claims of

women does not lie with *men*, for even those most opposed to them might be won over. Still less is it with *busy* women, for it has never happened to me yet to meet a woman who had done much work in the world as a philanthropist, artist, litterateur, or landed proprietor, who did not emphatically endorse the demand for the removal of those political disabilities which she had surely found at one point or another clog her steps. But the great obstacle lies with *idle* women, and nearly exclusively with those for whom nobody dreams of asking for the franchise – for the wives of rich men who have never known a want unsupplied, who have been surrounded by tenderness and homage from their cradles, and have lived all their days like little birds in a downy nest, with nothing to do but to open their beaks and find food dropped into them. It is to the eternal disgrace of such women that, instead of feeling burning shame and indignation at the wrongs and hardships which (as every newspaper shows them) their poorer sisters undergo, they think that, because the world is easy for *them*, it is 'the best of all possible worlds,' and that nothing ought to be changed in it. Like Marie Antoinette, they tell those who want bread to live on buns; and they extol the advantages of the 'chivalry' of men as ample compensation for the lack of every right, without once troubling themselves even to inquire whether the same 'chivalrous' gentleman, who hands them so courteously into a carriage, will not rudely brush past the shabby old governess, or call up the poor work-girl's blushes by his insolent address. When the

time comes – perhaps in this approaching Session –
when the doors of the Constitution will be opened once
more to welcome a new and still lower horde of Illiterates, by the assimilation of the County with the Borough
Franchise, we shall, doubtless, again hear the oft-
repeated assertion, that our legislators would gladly
extend the privilege to women if they believed they
really desired it; but that all the ladies whose opinions
they have asked, vehemently repudiate the proposal.
They might as well offer bread to an alderman at the
end of a feast, and, because he declines it, refuse it to a
pauper begging at the gate.

But, in spite of the rich and idle wives; and in spite of
the men who think the archetypal woman was – not a
Monkey – but a Doll; in spite of every obstacle, public
Sentiment is unquestionably slowly veering round, and
it depends on women themselves to bring it altogether
to their favour. In this, as in all other things, however,
to *be* is a much more important matter than to *do*. The
walls of modern Jerichos do not fall down by any trum-
peting outside, and the more women shriek for the
franchise, or for anything else, the less will men be disposed to open their ears to that extremely unpleasant
sound. Let us cease to be silly, and affected, and idle.
When we are ignorant, let us cultivate the grace of
silence; and when we adorn ourselves, let us do so by
the light of the 'Lamps' of Truth and Simplicity. This
achieved in the first place, let us become steady, diligent
sharers in the world's work, creeping up by degrees as
we prove our fitness for one higher task after another;

never for a moment asking or wishing to have allowance made for our defects, or over-estimation of our success 'because we are women.' When a sufficient number of us have taken this method of gaining public Sentiment to favour the claims of our sex, the victory will be assured. We may lay by our darts and catapults. The Simoon will blow quite in the opposite direction.

The House of Commons and Women's Suffrage

Sir, – The outcome of last Wednesday's Debate in the House of Commons is that the representatives of the people preferred to spend three hours in useless talk on an insignificant and repulsive subject, rather than be called upon to say Aye or No on the question of making further progress with the Women's Suffrage Bill. This is a new illustration, if one were wanted, of the difficulty and disadvantage at which any unrepresented section of the community stands when it asks for the time and attention of the Representative Chamber. Time is wasted, the dignity of Parliament is sacrificed, rather than give any attention to the wants and wishes of women. We have no votes, and, therefore, can safely be neglected and treated with contempt by Parliament.

The occurrences of last Wednesday will not fail, we imagine, to make this clear to many who have not seen it before, and if this be so we shall eventually gain rather than lose by what has taken place. May we venture, also, to put a question before your readers? Why do the opponents of Women's Suffrage in the House of Commons seek above all things to avoid a direct vote upon the subject? We cannot think that it is a symptom of conscious strength on their part. It appears as if Members of Parliament were beginning to be obliged to think of their Constituencies in this matter. We have no votes, but there are a considerable number of those who have who are convinced that justice and reason are favourable to the claim of women to representation. Members of Parliament, too, on all sides have encouraged the political activity of women during contested elections. It is not easy to do this and to say at the same time that women ought never to have the power to give a vote themselves.

The events of last Wednesday will stimulate our Societies to renewed activity: they illustrate our case for the representation of women. With its lessons fresh in all minds we shall appeal to the feelings of justice and fair play which animate the majority of our countrymen; and perhaps the Jubilee rejoicings may also have a share in convincing them that women are not necessarily, on account of their sex, unworthy to be trusted with political responsibility.

We are, Sir, your obedient servants,
M. M. RUSSELL COOKE.
MILLICENT GARRETT FAWCETT.
LILIAS ASHWORTH HALLETT.

The House of Commons and Women's Suffrage

KATHLEEN LYTTLETON.

PRISCILLA BRIGHT MCLAREN.

July 10.
London Evening Standard, 12 July 1897.

Speeches by Members of the Women's Social and Political Union

Miss Christabel Pankhurst:

Ladies & Gentlemen: The resolution has reference to the Bill which is now before Parliament, for the Enfranchisement of Women, and it is our intention during the whole of the present session to press for the enactment of that Bill, in order that, when the General Election comes – and I think that General Election is not now far distant – ('hear hear') women may have the opportunity as well as men of recording their opinions at the polling booth. Friends, every attempt has been made to make the second reading of that measure as spiritless and an ineffective thing, but I think it is within our power to rescue the Bill from the difficult position in which it stands, and compel the Government to carry this measure into law.

When the Bill was before the House, we had from Mr Herbert Gladstone a long speech of advice. What he said was that men had to struggle for centuries for their rights, since the days of Cromwell the fight had been going on – and still it was not completely won. Then he said experience shows that predominance of argument alone – and he believed that had been obtained – is not enough to win the political day. The time comes says Mr Gladstone, when political dynamics are? far those numbers (great applause) so that for all this the cry has been silenced that women do not want the vote.

The third and final announcement is with regard to tomorrow's arrangements. We shall not have a procession from Holloway Prison, we shall go straight to the Great Central Hotel in order to attend the Welcolm [*sic*] Breakfast to our released prisoners. When the breakfast is over, there will be a procession in which I hope as many as possible will join, to the Peckham Division, where a By-Election is in progress (great applause). Now, for some unknown reason – well, it may be a reason not unconnected with the Peckham contest – the Government have decided to release unexpectedly Mrs Pankhurst, and the other prisoners who were with her (applause) and therefore she is able to occupy the chair at tonight's meeting (tremendous applause, and pause for two or three minutes).

Mrs [Emmeline] Pankhurst:

Friends, this morning I was in Prison! (laughter) And I was thinking of this meeting here tonight, how in the solitude of my prison cell, while you women here were demanding your political freedom, my thoughts would be with you.

At two o'clock, the chief wardress came into my cell. She said 'You are to go out', and I said 'My time is not up until tomorrow morning. By whose authority am I to leave the prison?' She said 'There is an order for your release, and I suppose your friends procured it for you.'

(laughter) 'Not my friends', I said. Well we had to come out. Was it because the Government knew that we and you would be disappointed if we could not be here tonight, was it out of kindness that they did it? Well, one can hardly think so, because if they had felt that it wasn't fair to put political prisoners, who have broken no law, in the second division in solitary confinement ('shame') to deprive them of paper and pen and pencil, to deprive them even from speaking to one another, I think the order for our release would have come earlier than the day before the law entitled us to have it. No, I suppose they chose the lesser of two evils, they thought they preferred one Demonstration to two (laughter and applause). So I think we may conclude that is the reason why my friends and I, who should have been sleeping in Holloway tonight, are at this meeting with you. Well, while we have been in prison, you outside have been doing magnificent work. The Bill – because these things filter even into prison – the Bill has passed, after many years, its second reading. Well that is something, but you women have not studied Parliamentary procedure any more than some of the young Liberal MPs, [you] must not think too much of the second reading of the Women's Suffrage Bill. We know, who understand Parliamentary procedure, that that means little or nothing, that if we ever get beyond that state we women must do ten times more than we have done in the past to secure that the Bill shall successfully come to a third reading. While we have been in prison, I learn you have had two by-elections. One is over, and a great defeat to the Liberal

Government, the second is not concluded, so we women who proverbially are pushing will be pushing still until we know the result, but I understand that tomorrow we are to go along there, we women who have been in solitude so long, and do what we can to inflict upon the Government another defeat ('hear hear'). I understand that members of the Government have been saying that we must demonstrate as men did before they got the vote. Well, the night before I came to London, we had a demonstration in Yorkshire, on the historic site of the great Franchise Demonstration in the sixties. On Hunstead Moor in Leeds thousands of men demonstrated when they were agitating for the Franchise. The night before I came up to London for the Women's Parliament, we women had a procession in Leeds. Well, I think the whole of Leeds joined in the procession ('hear hear'). After the procession, with torches, we met on Hunstead Moor where Mr Herbert Gladstone had advised us to meet, and old men in Leeds who remembered that agitation said that never in the history of any agitation for reform had so many people congregated together on Hunstead Moor as met there that night (applause). But we women, because we are women, must do far more than the men ever did, to show that we are determined to gain their citizen rights. So I am glad to think that this programme for the summer months has been made, which if carried out successfully will prove to the satisfaction even of members of the Government that women indeed want the Vote, and mean to have it (great applause). And we may well be ready to spare no effort in our determination to get the Vote.

For more than fifty years, women have been demanding that common elementary right. We have always needed the Vote, we have always wanted it, but never so much as we need it today. Today we have the new kind of politics, very different from the old fashioned politics – because today politics means, as it never has meant before, interference with us all in our daily lives ('hear hear'). You have proposals out of Parliament, and in Parliament, for the regulation of our lives as we have never had before. No doubt with the best intentions – every body intends well – but we women need new representation in order to see that this new kind of legislation is not to be worse tyranny and a greater oppression than any kind of legislation that has gone before ('hear hear'). They say women have no sense of humour (laughter) but if it were not too [?so] serious, what is being done by men would create a sense of humour in women (applause and laughter). I am sorry if some of the gentlemen in the audience may feel their susceptibilities wounded by what I am going to say now (a man: 'No!') but to a woman it is humorous to see how men seem to think they are fitted to deal with questions which ever since the human race existed have been left to women to manage, and which women understand (great applause). How children, even, are to be brought into the world men in Parliament think they can decide now! The rearing and bearing of children, the care of the sick, the care of the old, the making of our homes, and the keeping of our homes, men are going to make laws to decide, without even giving us the elementary right of deciding who the men are to be who are to make these momentous decisions! (Applause) I need only give you one instance. This bill which the Government is introducing to decide the question of the controls of that splendid body of women who nurse the sick in our hospitals, rules and regulations are to be made for them, without even thinking it necessary to ask experienced women what these rules and regulations are to be (cries of 'unfair'). Well, I for one friends, looking round at the muddles men have made ('hear hear' – from men) looking round now at the starving children, looking round now at the sweated and decrepit members of my sex, I say men have had the control of these things long enough ('hear hear') and no woman with any spark of womanliness in her will consent to let this state of things go on any longer ('hear hear'). So this year we are going to settle the business ('hear hear'). We are tired and we want to be of use, we want to have this power in order that we may try to make this world a much better place for men and women than it is today. So I appeal to you women in this magnificent auditorium, every one of you to do your part. You need not go to prison. Yet I believe if you all did, as we have done – and it doesn't need much courage as some of you think – if you all made up your minds to do it, we would only have to do it once ('hear hear' and applause). Well we have got this programme planned out. You are going to hear more about it from other speakers because I have been shut away so I don't understand the details as fully, I cannot tell you as much about it as they can, but I know this, that we cannot carry out this programme, which means the bringing together of 150,000 determined women in June, unless we have the wherewithal to do it. Now politicians know better than women, because we are new to practical politics many of us, how much it costs in time and energy and money to carry out an agitation like this, but let me tell you this, that we want you all, we want your services, we want your energy, we want your time, we want your help, we want your money (laughter) and after all that is the least part of it ('hear hear' and applause). So in conclusion, I want to say I am very glad to be here tonight ('hear hear' and great applause). It makes me very happy to see what a few years ago I thought I should never live to see. They said 'You will never rouse women'. Well, we have done what they thought, and what they hoped ('hear hear') impossible – we women are roused ('hear hear' and great applause). Perhaps it is difficult to rouse women, and they are longsuffering and patient, now that we are roused, we will never be quiet again (great applause). There is a resolution to be put to the meeting later on, and it is my duty to move it from the chair. It is as follows:

'This meeting of women assembled in the Royal Albert Hall demand that constitutional rights be granted to women, and calls upon the government to adopt and carry into law the Women's Enfranchisement Bill now before Parliament.'

('hear hear' and applause) I move that resolution and

call upon Miss Annie Kenney, who at the opening of the London campaign, at a great Liberal Demonstration, from that box yonder, had the courage to put out a banner and say 'Will the Liberal Government give votes to women?'

I call upon Miss Annie Kenney to second the resolution (great applause).

Miss Annie Kenney:

Mrs Pankhurst, women of Great Britain, who are here to demand the ?just liberties of a nation, and who have a great consciousness of right at heart, I want to tell [?thank] you on behalf of Mrs Pankhurst and of those women who have been away, for your grand support, and for your true loyalty to this Union while we women were in prison. You do not know, you cannot understand what it means to we women workers and organisers of this Union, how full our hearts feel of joy, full of hope, full of confidence, and our souls full of inspiration, to see you support our great Women's Movement. I cannot help but feel glad to be once again in the Albert Hall. Almost two years ago when the Liberals of the country had decided to hold the meeting of the century in the Royal Albert Hall, we women of Manchester agreed with Mrs Pankhurst that one of we women [*sic*] ought to come to London, get tickets if humanly possible, come to the meeting, and see if Women's Franchise was included in the great reform. I was the one who was sent to be delegate from the Manchester branch. We were very fortunate – we always are – ('hear hear', and laughter) we got 4 tickets; two for

Mr John Burns' private Box – unknown to Mr Burns (laughter), and two for the orchestra. It was decided that one of the London women and I should occupy the box. The night came for the meeting, so I sent a letter to the leading Liberal man, saying that I was inside the Hall, that I hoped that Women's Suffrage would be treated in the manner that it well deserved and would be included in the great Liberal programme. I also said that, if it was not included in the programme, I should feel bound to get up and make a protest against its exclusion ('bravo' and applause). We women were like the Barons in the Saga of King John, we had sworn that the women of this country should have their political liberty, and that we as women would declare war against any Government that was run on unconstitutional lines (applause). We have done it (laughter). Now, you all know that women's suffrage was not included in the programme. So, when I saw the speakers were getting to the end of their speeches I got up in the box, when they were telling of the great reforms that the Liberals were going to do, and I said to them 'Are you going to give women the Vote?' The whole hall seemed to rise and much to the dismay of Mr John Burns and his friends I pulled out my banner from under my cloak and hung it over the box (great applause). I shall never forget the scene. There seemed to be thousands of people against me, but I didn't mind, because I knew that we had done the right thing, and I knew that our action that night was like summer rain on a drooping flower, it would give new life new spirit to the women's movement in London, and is not this meeting one of the many proofs that we women were right ('yes' and 'hear hear').

One cannot help but wonder all about the old reformers who have gone by, and I often wonder what they must have felt about their reforms, what they must have felt about their movements, and knowing that every reform that strove for liberty, that worked against oppression and slavery, that worked for the up-lifting of the human race, was won more through pressure than from a sense of justice – was won at a price of human sacrifice and human life. Think how the men won their first Franchise Reform; think how the Merchants Shipping Bill was won to save thousands of honest seamen from death; think how the first Factory Acts were won, to protect lives of our little children against the greed of employers, and save their little bodies from this cruel machine; think of all the strife and loss of life before the government of that day would recognise the need of combination between the workers to protect their interests. The strife of those days won for us the liberties we now enjoy, the strife of today will win liberty and freedom for the generations that are to come ('hear hear' and applause). I do not think when the battle is won we shall ever have cause to regret all the uphill work that had to be done, but we shall rather think of what we should have missed had we got our Vote without a great struggle for it. We should not have had, we should not have known our dear leader Mrs Pankhurst ('hear hear' and applause), we should not have known our champion, Miss Christabel Pankhurst (great applause), we should not have had our treasure of treasurers, Mrs Pethick Lawrence and I should have been far poorer without them. They would not have had you good women, there would not have been the grand fellowship existing between the women of every class, of every creed, as there is today (applause). To the Liberal Party is the loss, to the women of our land will come the gain. Let us just look at the conditions the people of our land are living under today. Just think, and then be satisfied with life as it is if you can! Your prisons are full, your workhouses are overcrowded, your lunatic asylums are overcrowded: you have over thirteen million starving women, men and children – you have your thousands of underpaid, sweated women workers, and we want to consider what all this means to we women! Have you ever been in our British Institutions? Have you been in your workhouses and seen your old women packed together, just at the time of life when they should be made bright and comfortable for their old age, to give those tired hands and weary hearts a chance of rest? Have you ever been in our maternity wards? And seen our young girl mothers? Have you ever been in our imbecile wards, and seen the children that are borne of women, some of the children that are borne in sin? It would be wrong if the women were satisfied; it would be wrong if we women (great applause) it would be wrong if we women did not burn with righteous indignation. Where is our religion, where is our Christianity,

if we are prepared to stand by without lifting our hands to help? Let us look at the condition of our prisons . . .
    End of transcript.

Royal Albert Hall, 19 March 1908.

Suffragist Demonstration in Edinburgh

Something of a pageant, largely a procession, and wholly a spectacular advertisement, the women's franchise demonstration which took place in Edinburgh on Saturday afternoon will be remembered as a great success from the point of view of its promoters, the Women's Social and Political Union. Everything was in its favour. Better weather conditions could not have been chosen; the streets were in perfect condition; and although the southerly breeze may have troubled standard-bearers, it was agreeable to the enormous crowds who came to witness the scene. [. . .]

It would be impossible to estimate their numbers, but a fair proportion of the city's population must have been present on the route. Interest in the show was keen, but of other feeling – enthusiasm for example – there was none. Occasionally there was a slight vocal exhibition of hostility, and once in the vicinity of Castle Terrace a bag of peasemeal burst over the heads of the immediate lady processionists. At intervals where groups of sympathisers had assembled there was cheering and some waving of handkerchiefs. But the vast majority of the onlookers exhibited no other sentiment than that of mere curiosity [. . .]

There was a perfect forest of bannerettes; there were quantities of inscribed banners carried on two poles; and there was quite a selection of imposing standards, which had to be entrusted to stout masculine arms. All were in the suffragist colours – purple, white and green. The triple tints were everywhere. Many of the women wore purple hats, with green or purple dresses, and white sashes with the inscribed words, 'Votes for women.' Immense labour had been expended on the banners and standards. No two banners had the same inscription, and many of the mottos were smart and *apropos*. 'What's guid for John is guid for Janet' had its obvious hit. One, devoted to Mr Asquith, said 'Ye maunna tramp on the Scotch thistle, laddie.' Others read: – 'He who's for us, for him are we'; 'Cry all together, that's the way to be served'; 'The langest day has an end'; and 'Nae gain without pain.' Apart from the eighteen tableaux which had been arranged, there was no great attempt at costume effect. A number of girl graduates wore their gown and trencher, and several richly lined silk hoods indicated that their wearers had taken their degree. One group of fisher girls in their short kirtles made a notable variation. The great mass of the processionists belonged to the middle class, and they were evidently much in earnest.

The most active person at the Links was Mrs [Flora] Drummond, the principal marshal of the procession. She appeared on horseback, and she rode astride. She wore a flat cap in the suffragist colours, and a long green overcoat, divided from the waist. An attendant cavalier on foot was prepared to assist her if she got into difficulties with the horse, but she had it under perfect control. When the procession was about to start she invited the public to fall in, but the invitation did not seem to be anywhere accepted. A number of other ladies appeared on horseback, but only one of them adopted Mrs Drummond's mode of riding. The remainder, who included Lady Steel and the Hon. Mrs Haverfield, rode the orthodox side saddle, and were gowned in the riding habit. [. . .]

All the tableaux, scattered judiciously among the processionists, were representative of women whose deeds have become historic, or of scenes in which women took heroic part. There were none but were worthy of attention, and several of them were particularly effective. A striking figure on horseback was the Fair Lilliard, who fought at Ancrum Moor. The Fair Lilliard was represented by a pretty brunette, who wore a plain metal headpiece, a coat painted in realistic fashion to represent silver armour, and a flowing mauve skirt. The Countess Buchan created much attention in her grim-looking cage set upon a lorry. – On the lorry was the inscription, 'Confined in a cage outside Berwick Castle for crowning Bruce when no man dared.' A lorry with a tragic burden was that which bore the representatives of the two Solway martyrs, who were drowned for the sake of their religion. They both appeared tied to stakes, and one whose hair fell loosely round her shoulders had a particularly dramatic air. Among other notable personages were Mary Queen of Scots; Devorgilla, who founded

Balliol College and built Dumfries Bridge; Jenny Ged-
des, who had a model of the historic stool on the lorry
with her; Midside Maggie, who baked the bannock
enclosing the gold which enabled the Earl of Lauderdale
to escape; Lady Grisel Bailey, Flora Macdonald, Helen
Macgregor, and others. [. . .]

When the first of the processionists arrived at the
Waverley Market few persons were inside the large hall,
which had been specially fitted up for the accommo-
dation of the suffragists and their supporters [. . .]
Punctually at four o'clock, Mrs Pankhurst and the other
members of the platform party took their seats on the
platform. The company in the reserved area rose from
their seats and gave the speakers a rousing welcome.
Mingled with the cheering, however, was a considerable
volume of booing from the back of the hall.

Mrs Pankurst, who took the chair, apparently found
the acoustics of the hall to trouble her, for she began her
speech in strained and strident tones. Frequent though
the interruptions were from the rear, they did not interfere with her flow of oratory, and she continued her
address with vigour. 'Lead, Kindly Light' was at one
time struck up by the noisy section. Amid the din Mrs
Pankhurst held forth, and concluded by moving a resolution expressing 'profound indignation at the recent
disgraceful development of the Government's policy of
coercion towards women are demanding that taxation
and representation should go together' and calling upon
the Government 'to put an end to this deplorable struggle by giving the vote to duly qualified women.'

Mrs Pethick Lawrence, who was the next speaker, roused the antagonism of the noisy section of the audience by her references to the presence of supporters of the Government, and her declaration that the women on the platform were far better Liberals than the interrupters. She had not proceeded far before the uproar became so great that her voice was drowned. A good deal of jostling went on behind the barriers at the rear of the hall, and many in the reserved area, unable to hear a word of the speaker, rose in their seats to ascertain the cause of the disturbance. Mrs Pankhurst intervened, and counselled the audience not to trouble about 'a handful of irresponsible boys.' The 'irresponsible boys', however, were not so easily put down. They apparently made an attempt to rush the barrier placed round the reserved seats, and a large number of ladies who were in the vicinity were badly crushed. The stewards, who were inside the barriers, were unable for the moment to quell the disturbance, and a large force of police which had been in reserve outside the building made their appearance. They took up positions among the rowdy section, and the disturbance quickly ceased. Several young men who had been in the thick of the row left the hall. At this stage Mrs Drummond announced from the platform that it was not on the authority of the Union that the police were called in. She said that she refused to allow the police to turn out the disturbers.

Mrs Lawrence thereafter proceeded with her speech, which was listened to without further interruption.

Appeals for Scottish support for the movement were

made by Mrs Pankhurst and Mrs Drummond; and after a collection was taken, an address in support of the resolution was delivered by Miss Christabel Pankhurst, who declared that they did not come there to apologise for their brave comrades in Newcastle, but to boast of them.

The resolution was carried by an overwhelming majority, the dissenters numbering about a score.

Led by Mrs Drummond, who waved her riding whip, the audience gave three cheers for the pioneers of the movement, and for the prisoners at present in jail.

Extract from *The Scotsman*, 11 October 1909.

The Women's Suffrage Movement among Trade Unionists

EVA GORE-BOOTH

Lancashire and Cheshire Women Textile and other Workers Representation Committee.

July, 1904.

Fellow Workers. – During the last few years the need of political power for the defence of the workers has been felt by every section of the labour world. Among the men the growing sense of the importance of this question has resulted in the formation of the Labour Representation Committee with the object of gaining direct Parliamentary Representation for the already enfranchised working men. Meanwhile the position of the unenfranchised working women, who are by their voteless condition shut out from all political influence, is becoming daily more precarious. They cannot hope to hold their own in industrial matters, where their interests may clash with those of their enfranchised fellow-workers or employers.

The one all-absorbing and vital political

question for labouring women is to force an entrance into the ranks of responsible citizens, in whose hands lie the solution of the problems which are at present convulsing the industrial world.

In view of the complicated state of modern politics, and the mass of conflicting interests, the conclusion has been forced on those of the textile workers who have been working unceasingly in past years to secure the votes for women, that what is urgently needed is that they should send their own nominee to the House of Commons, pledged to work in season and out of season to secure the enfranchisement of the women workers of the country.

A committee has been formed of women in the trade from various Lancashire and Cheshire towns, whose duties are (1) to select a suitable and zealous candidate, and (2) to collect and be responsible for the spending of £500, which is the amount absolutely necessary for one candidate's election expenses. A balance sheet will be submitted to each town subscribing.

Any one who wishes to better the position of her fellow-workers, and the thousands of women outside the ranks of the skilled cotton operatives, who are being overworked and underpaid, should remember that political enfranchisement must precede industrial emancipation, and that the political disabilities of women have done incalculable harm, by cheapening their labour and lowering their position in the industrial world.

What Lancashire and Cheshire Women think to-day England will do to-morrow.

Yours fraternally,

Pro The Committee:
SARAH DICKINSON,
SELINA COOPER,
SARAH REDDISH,
ESTHER ROPER,
EVA GORE-BOOTH.

So ran the manifesto of the Lancashire Textile Workers in 1904, when, after years of patient work on the old lines, they came to the conclusion it was time to adopt newer and more forcible methods. In 1901 and 1902, petitions signed by 67,000 textile workers had been taken to the House of Commons by deputations of women employed in the trade, deputations of enthusiastic workers who could not believe in the indifference of the well-to-do world to the claims of unenfranchised wage-earners, and came back to Lancashire sadder and wiser women. A good deal of stir had begun inside the Cotton Unions, and, in various towns, votes were taken as to whether Women's Suffrage was to be a Trade Union question. It was felt by the women that the Cotton Unions should make a practical effort to secure the benefits of political enfranchisement for their 96,000 women members. It is noteworthy that, wherever this vote was taken (Bolton, Clitheroe, Colne, Nelson, Hyde, Haslingden), majorities of over 1,000 decided in favour of immediate action, and there were but few dissentients. The Burnley Weavers' Union specially instructed their Committee to bring the matter before the Trade Congress.

For many years, enthusiastic meetings and demonstrations had been held in all the great Northern towns and centres of industry. The matter was one very familiar to the working people. For it will easily be understood that a grievance that is hardly felt by women of money, and position, and influence, may become well nigh intolerable in its practical bearing on the lives of those who are industrially an independent force, and politically the helpless toy of the amateur philanthropist, of the exploiter of cheap labour, and of that narrow spirit of exclusion and oppression that is bred among the very workers themselves by the severity of our present industrial competitive system. As time went on, and as the political power to which they were admitted in 1868 assumed more and more importance in the minds of working men, the question of the women's enfranchisement became more and more prominent amongst working people.

The climate of thought in England is not tropical. We are not subject to sudden cataclysms and earthquakes and cyclones. We pride ourselves on the absence of sudden and violent Revolutions, and on the slow growth and gradual fruition of our political ideas. During the last fifty years a great change has taken place in the minds of the more progressive working people, a change that was observed in the making by some of our more long-sighted politicians, notably Lord Randolph

Churchill. 'The Labour community is carrying on at the present day a very significant and instructive struggle . . . It realises that it now possesses political power to such an extent as to make it independent of either party in the State; the struggle it is carrying on is one . . . for the practical utilisation in its own interest of the great political power it has acquired. The Labour interest is now seeking to do for itself what the landed interest and the manufacturing interest did for themselves . . . We are now come, or are coming fast, to a time when Labour Laws will be made by the Labour interest for the advantage of Labour. The regulation of all the conditions of Labour by the State controlled and guided by the Labour vote appears to be the ideal aimed at.'

Strangely enough, when the Labour Representation movement began to make itself felt in Lancashire, it was by the votes of women that it stood or fell. For there is one thing that women are usually allowed to vote, and that is their money (unless, of course, it is taken from them by the autocratic will of Parliament). Those progressive people who would deny votes to women for the statesman-like reason that they were supposed to vote Conservative in the London County Council election, would do well to place beside this hypothesis the incontestable fact that before the Cotton Unions could subscribe £900 a year to the Labour Representation Committee, and before a candidate could be run and his salary paid as Labour candidate for Clitheroe, a ballot had to be taken of the women who far outnumbered the men in the Unions. The women did not grudge their money for Labour Representation, and at the time Mr Shackleton himself pointed out how large a part of the burden fell on the shoulders of these unrepresented workers. When Mr Shackleton was returned unopposed for Parliament in 1902, 5,500 women trade unionists in the Clitheroe division petitioned him to bring forward and press on the Women's Franchise question so that they too might share in the benefits of Parliamentary Representation. Then came a period of apathy on the men's part to the women's claims, a period during which the unpleasant truth gradually soaked into these women's minds that those who had been their equals and comrades in industry, had passed wholly out of their sphere of influence, and were as deaf to the appeals of the politically helpless as were the 'princes' in whom the working men of old time 'put their trust.' Among the Lancashire working women there is a strong inherent sense of commercial honesty and personal independence, and it is no exaggeration to say that among the more progressive workers there has grown up a deep feeling of bitterness and disappointment, a feeling which culminated this year when the Labour Party, led away by a theoretic inclination for the very stale red-herring of immediate complete and entire adult suffrage, refused to fulfil their written pledge and press forward a measure for the enfranchisement of women. It is apparently a very easy matter for men to muddle the issues with high-sounding protests against the terms of their own enfranchisement, a measure by which they do not themselves refuse to profit. Their position is absolutely indefensible. They have built up the whole of the Labour Party on what they are pleased to call a property qualification, a qualification that gives votes to houses and lodgings, not to flesh and blood, a qualification that, according to their own often repeated statements, no democratic person could accept, or even compromise with as a temporary instalment of justice. If what these Labour men say is true, then it follows that the Labour Party is built in sin and founded on unrighteousness. If, on the other hand, what they say is not true, comment is surely superfluous. So far we have not observed amongst them any disinclination to use their own votes; nor do they even shrink from representing in Parliament thousands of arrogant enfranchised houses and politically emancipated lodgings without an effort to enfranchise poor enslaved flesh and blood. In fact, they have eaten their cake, and enjoyed and digested it; it is only when a hungry beggar asks for a slice that they find out that it is poisonous.

The working women had answered to the Labour appeal; they had supported with their votes and money the new movement for what they had fondly dreamt was the representation of working people, and now they understand that those workers who are most in need of the protection of the franchise are still to be outside the pale. They do not undervalue the kind offices of individual friends, but it is a Party they supported in the time of need generously, and on a large scale, and it is to that Party that they appeal. 'Be just before you are generous,' is the simplest appeal in the world, and surely it is the fundamental basis of all right doing and political honesty.

It is easy to blame the Lancashire women for their reckless confidence. Certainly they scattered their bread on the waters with a princely disregard of consequences. There is a curious power in this world, the working of which we all of us feel instinctively, the force that Emerson called 'The Law of Compensation.' As much as you give out you draw in; what you pay the price for you earn.

Again, according to the philosopher, 'There is no god dare wrong a worm'; 'Power to him who power exerts.' The justice inherent in things always in the end asserts itself. If you cast your bread upon the waters, you shall most certainly find it again. But alas! that all these good hopes are only fulfilled 'after many days.' Surely the working women of England have paid the price of political emancipation over and over again! It is no mere insignificant statistical fact that these millions of workers live laborious days of poverty-stricken and upright independence, and produce by their labour so large a proportion of the material wealth of the country. Here is a force that must in the end be reckoned with. 'Power to him who power exerts.' We know of course that it is only a question of time; that there is no government in the world, however autocratic, that can in the end keep five millions of its responsible workers out of all political rights whatsoever. 'Great is the truth and shall prevail,' says Coventry Patmore; 'when no man care if it prevail or no.' This, at all events, does not seem likely, for the working women's representatives get more and more urgent in their appeal. Every month and every year that this measure of justice is denied to us, the condition of the working women becomes more and more desperately difficult. In fact, we are bound to care more, not less; and this for a very simple reason: Every year that goes by sees the slow development of the tendency to nationalise all industrial questions. Political and industrial issues can be no longer disentangled. The very trade unions that forty years ago shouted down their more progressive members with cries of 'No politics,' are now running candidates of their own at elections. Industrial questions are gradually shifting their ground and becoming political questions, and, as this happens, the working women are more and more beginning to feel the disadvantage of not being able to enter the sphere where questions connected with their bread and butter and hours of labour and weekly income are fought out.

Anybody who studies with an impartial mind the industrial position of women in England must surely come to the conclusion that there is something radically wrong and unfair in that position. To begin with, wherever they are employed, with few exceptions, they are paid at lower rates than could be offered to men, and their work is restricted to the poorer and lesser paid parts of those trades. In fact, they get all the kicks and none of the halfpence. And when they have gone home with the wretched 7s. or 10s. which they are forced by hunger to accept for wages, they are bitterly reproached by men for undercutting, and for 'having a lower standard of comfort than men.' This low rate of wages among women is, of course, not due to original sin, or to some strange sex aberration which makes them unable to understand the usefulness of money. Neither is it due to want of organisation. There are thirty thousand women members of the National Union of Teachers, and yet, under every Education Committee in England, there is a reasoned-out scale by which every girl pupil-teacher is paid less than every boy pupil-teacher. And this principle is carried through right up to the head-masters and headmistresses, irrespective of qualifications or training. Even in the cotton trade, which is, I suppose, the best trade for women in England, and where there are ninety-six thousand women in the Unions, the average is quoted by Miss Collet (Board of Trade) as 14s. a week, a sum far below the wage of even an unskilled labouring man. In this connection the experiences of the men are somewhat illuminating. During the last sixty years, Mr Sidney Webb points out, the wages of working men have increased by 50 to 100 per cent., whilst the wages of working women have remained stationary or grown less. Since their enfranchisement the agricultural labourers have been able to increase their wages largely, in spite of the fact of their Union falling to pieces.

The present tendency of Government to involve itself more and more in direct industrial enterprise has caused great enthusiasm among progressive politicians, who welcome it as a way of securing good industrial conditions for thousands of working men. Beyond this again, as Mr Sidney Buxton pointed out last year, the Government, as the biggest employer of labour in the country, exerts a very great, if indirect, influence on the whole labour market. Thus the men workers are in the position, not only of having their biggest employers elected by public election, but one of the great forces that react on the male labour market is also at the mercy of public election. The Trade Unionist politicians were right to congratulate themselves. They are able to keep up the rate by unceasing vigilance and application of political pressure in the House of Commons, with the result that Government is a model employer for men. But not for women. In the evidence before the Royal Commission on the Wages of Postal Servants, it is very clearly shown how the Government wages for clerks are lower than those given by other employers. Lancashire employers are able to give weavers the same rate whether they are men or women, but everywhere in Government employment wages are carefully calculated according to sex and not work. So that, in the Pimlico Clothing Factory, the skilled woman worker gets an average of 15s. a week, while no man labourer gets less than 23s. The Government mechanically gets its female labour as cheap as it can, unchecked by political considerations. The example spreads to public boards and private employers, who cannot afford to be undercut by one another, and thus their political weakness first depresses the wages of thirty thousand women, and then, through them, depresses the standard of women's remuneration all over the country.

I once heard a learned Professor assert with beautiful simplicity to a crowd of tailoresses earning about 7s. a week each, 'Your low wages are due to yourselves. Perhaps, some day, if you work very well, you may be worth 14s. a week.' This was, no doubt, a comforting doctrine for the Professor, whose salary could not have been less than £400 a year. But I think most people must realise nowadays that your payment is not so much for what you do, and its value to the world, but for what you are. The parlour-maid may be a better worker and a more valuable servant than the footman, but he gets higher wages for being a man.

Social barriers are growing less and less amongst men, since the working men have become the ruling political force in the nation, but still, you will find that a Foreign Office clerk, without any Trade Union at all, is able to get a higher rate of pay for his work than an engine-driver or skilled engineer, however valuable his services may be to the community, and in spite of the fact that he belongs to one of the strongest Trade Unions in England. A Government clerk may be a very valuable member of society, but the proportion of his salary to the wages of the engineer is hardly accounted for by a correspondingly lower rate of utility in the engineer's highly skilled work. If you want to increase a person's industrial value, you must increase his importance, you must make it worth somebody's while to please him. A hundred years ago the working men had no political

importance, and they suffered from fining and low
wages exactly in the same way that women do now. It
is not one party or the other party that has improved
their position, it is the pressure of the working men's
votes on all parties. In practical life, these things are not
doubted by working men. 'My opinion should have
some weight,' said the Weavers' Secretary at a Lancashire Trade Council meeting, 'for I represent by far the
biggest Union in the town.' 'What's the good of your
Union?' said the Engineers' Secretary, 'why, it's all
women; mine mayn't be large, but, at all events, they're
voters.' One vote more or less may be a matter of small
importance, but an organised industrial Union of voters
is a weapon of real political force, and the possession of
this weapon makes society very sensitive to the grievances and claims of the band of workers who are so well
equipped. There are some people nowadays who still
see the world in water-tight compartments. They will
tell you that industrial results are due to economic
causes, political results to political causes, social results
to social causes. But we have seen a war a great political
event that was undoubtedly the result of economic
causes; we have watched every Factory Act that passes
the House of Commons become more and more fraught
with consequences to the industrial lives of women; we
have seen indeed the gradual widening of the social
chasm between the men who have emerged into political power and position, and their women comrades
who are still washing dishes and cooking dinners. And
we realise that all the arbitrary limits between the

political and industrial world are only limits of the imagination. They do not, in fact, exist. Few people will deny that money is power; the discovery of this generation of English people, the discovery which is gradually working its way into the minds of the poor, is that power is money. Industry, society, politics, there is one magic key that opens the doors of prosperity in all the worlds, and that key is power. In the case of the working women, they have to break through a vicious circle of political disability working itself out in industrial weakness and social impotence. There are many causes given for the low rates earned by women, and doubtless many factors go to decide the vexed question of wages; but I venture to assert that there is not one of them that you can impartially examine and not find that it is but a new form behind which masquerades the ancient and ubiquitous fact of the political subjection of women. It is unjust of people to reproach us with the fact that we are people of one idea. Because it is not we who follow the idea, but the idea that follows us. It dogs our footsteps wherever we go. In the mills and workshops, it regulates our lives and depresses our wages. It holds the constant threat of abolition and starvation over the heads of those who work in their own homes. It follows us on to the pit brow, and waits for us vindictively on all licensed premises, even showing its face in the harmless railway restaurants, and scaring the poor manageress who has attained a position of responsibility through hard work. It walks abroad among the variety artistes, and thinks nothing of proposing that ten thousand people should be turned out of their work because, contrary to human experience in that profession, they might break their legs. It arranges the education of children, and the hours of labour – the poor woman can never escape from the harassing experiences of her subjection.

As regards the more educated classes, it stands as a lion in the path between them and the higher branches of the professions, or the recognition of their abilities.

But it must never be forgotten that the sufferings of the poor are the most urgent sufferings because, though the opportunities of educated women may be stunted, and their careers spoilt and their ambitions thwarted, they can at least possess their own souls' light, and, like Wordsworth's 'forgotten taper,' to the last 'drive from themselves all frightful gloom,' whilst the very life itself of the poor is stunted by that terrible struggle with poverty that leaves them, too often, neither leisure nor energy nor physical strength enough for self-development or education or the joy of life.

This is what the Trade Union women realised when, in 1904, the Women's Textile Committee and the Manchester and Salford Women's Trade and Labour Council laid their plans for the General Election. The need of strong and effective action had been brought home to them by recent events. They decided on a wholly new policy. They were not Party women; they would take up and use the only real political weapon that it is in the power of women to use at present. They would lead the way in a new warfare; they would choose a constituency and fight an election in the interests of the working women's franchise against all comers. They would appeal from party feeling to the industrial knowledge and sympathy of working women. People said they would not get five votes. They said then they would do with four, and always they hoped that this election would be the beginning of a new movement. They would try again and again, no matter how few votes they got, and then other women would join in the fray, and by degrees the idea would spread and Women's Suffrage candidates would be brought forward in all the bye-elections.

When they went to Wigan the expected happened, and they were repudiated by all parties and sections. They appealed from the parties and organisations to the men at the mills and factories and workshops and mines and football fields. After a fortnight's work of twenty women and three men, unsupported by parties or organisations, a vote of 2,200 was gained by Mr Thorley Smith, the women's candidate, and he was second at the poll in a three-cornered fight. Thus our appeal is from the Government to the nation, from the House of Commons to the electors, from the rich to the poor.

The rich may say that 'women should stay at home and cook the dinner'; the poor know that if women did stay at home there would often be no dinner to cook. The Government says, 'We have nothing to do with you, you can bring no pressure to bear on us'; but the nation says, 'We feel the pressure of your poverty.' In spite of the deafness and blindness of the political parties to human needs, working men everywhere are beginning to realise that the exclusion from all political rights of a body of 5,000,000 workers is not only a source of industrial weakness and poverty to themselves, but a danger to the whole of the world of labouring people.

1909

The Civic Rights of the Married Woman

CONSTANCE SMEDLEY

It is universally acknowledged that marriage and motherhood are the woman's crown. From every point of view the married woman is considered a more mature, developed, and responsible being than the spinster; she is, moreover, the most precious possession of the nation, bearing and rearing, as she does, its children. A mother's instinct is held to be unerring; her sympathies are supposed to be wider and more humanised; her altruism is proverbial.

As a citizen all men would place her value higher than the unmarried woman who exists to support herself, however cultured and useful to the community the latter's intelligence may be. They know that her experience of life is necessarily deeper, and her judgment sounder; they know also the services which a good wife and mother renders to her nation are of the most supreme importance.

And yet here comes the extraordinary inconsistency. There are many men who support the plea of the working woman for her civic rights on the basis that she is a ratepayer, who yet absolutely dispute the justice of the clause which admits the married woman to a share of her husband's political responsibilities. They argue that the man pays the rent and taxes, and that to give his wife a vote would amount to giving him a double privilege for the sum he pays towards the nation's maintenance. This argument may be easily dismissed by the fact that representation is not granted according to the sum of money paid by the citizen. The millionaire who pays in thousands and the clerk who pays his £5 note have each one vote alike; each has the vote simply as a citizen, quite apart from the value of his personal possessions.

The second argument is, that it is unnecessary for the woman to have a voice; the man is the head of the household, and is quite competent of deciding for his household. He alone, therefore, has the right to an opinion on all questions of national importance, even though many of those questions peculiarly and personally affect women and children, and are therefore questions in the solving of which a woman's instinct and experience would be invaluable. When it is pointed out that the man of the household is not always the superior member of that household, morally or mentally, we are confronted with the argument that by giving the woman a vote we should give cause for terrible matrimonial dissension. Indeed, this threat of matrimonial trouble is voiced so frequently that it gives rise to a very shrewd suspicion on our part that a good many men know in their own hearts that their wives and mothers of their children would think very differently from them on certain matters, and especially as to the vital importance and urgency of certain matters.

It can hardly be disputed that woman's intelligence and practicality is equal in the main to man's. If there were such a thing as an electoral examination women would not complain of having to pass it; nor would the voting register show an amazing preponderance of masculine names.

Given two beings of equal intelligence, the plea of withholding the right to vote from one on the ground that she lacks an economic stake in the country, is rather a feeble one when applied to the woman who has often given up lucrative employment to look after a man's house, bear his children, and make a home for him and them. If such a woman trusts her husband too completely to ask for a settlement from him upon her marriage, and consequently freely gives the myriad services of a wife and mother, nurse and housekeeper, in exchange for a home alone, I do not see that it follows that she should be disqualified from having a voice in her own and her children's destinies, or from being directly represented in the Government which she must obey. If she is one of the most valuable of the nation's citizens she should have a voice in its affairs. The argument that a woman has quite sufficient to do in looking after her house and children without worrying her head about politics strikes at the mainspring of a nation's development. The mothers of the nation are, to some extent, responsible for the world into which they bring the children; they are not mere breeding animals. They must protect and guide their children; they also must protect themselves. Every law that has to do with education, sanitation, food, drink, housing, social questions, sexual relations, has to do directly with the wives and mothers who must obey such laws, and they are entitled to a direct voice in such matters just as much as any man. It cannot be too much insisted upon that motherhood is the strongest force in existence that makes for altruism, and altruism is the most essential factor in the wise and beneficial ordering of the State. The mother will not be biassed in favour of laws that press unduly on the male; for the welfare of her sons is as important to her as the welfare of her daughters; she is naturally in favour of all conditions that help to their moral strengthening and wholesome living, and because of the gift of motherhood she will feel most poignantly on all laws that touch upon the health and happiness of the children. Men know this; even those who jeer at women keep the saving grace of reverence for the mother who bore and nurtured them.

It may be said that I have a tendency to idealise women; that all mothers are not wise, nor tender, nor unselfish; that I forget, moreover, the wisdom and responsibility of the father. But I am not pleading that he should be disenfranchised, I only say that all fathers and husbands with a certain economic qualification have a vote. I would point out that the wives and mothers have an equal stake in the nation and contribute equally to its health and well-being.

But comes the cry of the frivolity of woman's

interests; and her indifference to political, and her apathy in municipal matters, are cited as proof of her incapacity of understanding.

I admit the frivolity of her present interests; but I would ask men to remember that it is they who push woman into the social whirlpool, by the mere fact of their eliminating all serious interests from her life as 'unwomanly.'

Husbands dislike their wives to meddle with politics or any other pursuit or profession which man has decided is his own peculiar affair: they prefer her to concentrate her thoughts on themselves, their home and children; to the feeding of them; the amusing of them. They want their wives to rest them, not to stimulate. They want to leave the sterner side of life, with its responsibilites and need of thought, behind them when they seek their fireside.

But do men ever reflect that while they consider it the woman's duty to eliminate everything from her thoughts which gives no pleasure to men, men themselves never consider it their duty to spend the whole of their time making their minds over to the pattern the woman would prefer for them to copy?

The wife, kept all day in her home, taught to concentrate her every thought on the charming and the pleasing of her husband, desires – naturally – constant proof and profession of his love from her husband. This exigency soon bores the husband. After the first few months of married life, his passion has quietened: he is no longer dominated by it. His business and political interests come back again: he does not want to spend his days in devotion to his wife. His club calls him; sport; his men friends. He resents his wife's appearance at his office to accompany him home. He insists on keeping his 'man's life' wholly separate and to himself.

He has no objection, therefore, to his wife 'calling' on her neighbours. Very kindly and reasonably he sees that she cannot be expected to stay at home all day long, performing the housework, so he grants her the relief of social interests: laughing, as he does, at the pettiness of the scheming, the small return of enjoyment from the expenditure, the heartburning, the jealousy, the hollowness and smallness of the social triumphs his wife is working for.

Still, it is all fit occupation for his womenfolk! No matter though social ambition often destroys the peace of the household, and leads women into extravagance which is an unwarrantable burden to lay upon the breadwinner! No man's voice is heard raised against the round of afternoon tea-parties, dinners, lunches, each more vapid than the other, as being an occupation unworthy of womanhood. No man bestows the epithet 'unsexed' upon the butterfly of fashion, who spends her days climbing up the social ladder, injuring other women ruthlessly, wasting her husband's money in the satisfaction of vulgar vanity and uncloaked greed! So long as she takes care of her æsthetic possibilities, preserves an inane mind devoid of any serious sentiment or thought, and continues chaste according to the letter of the law, man merely calls her 'feminine' and forgives her obvious failings with amazing indulgence.

It almost drives one to the conclusion that men not only do not expect women to be worth much, morally or intellectually, but they do not want them to be worth much. Only then one remembers man's reverence for womanhood and his ideal of a noble, altruistic, ministering angel!

Men must admit they are almost bafflingly inconsistent. They have a habit nowadays of decrying education and the consequently intellectual woman as the cause of racial suicide. Can men not see that irresponsibility in all the nation's affairs must have a bad effect; and that now woman's gain of freedom gives her a wider scope for amusement and a consequent greater love of change and excitement, her moral development must be encouraged by a fair share of moral and social responsibilities.

When her children grow up, go to school, marry, a woman's life is apt to become empty. Better surely that she seeks to help in the bettering of the conditions of society, than to waste her days in party-giving and frittering of her time in vapid 'calls' or purposeless shopping.

The modern woman has lost her sense of duty, so they say; rather has she lost the sense of blind obedience to the will of man. In the struggle to throw off the yoke, she only thought of being free. Now that she is comparatively free, her inherent sense of duty is welling up within her. So also is her sense of pity, of compassion and self-sacrifice. Wives and mothers want to help the State in its growth, in its happiness, in the opportunities it gives its citizens for their development.

Why does man seek to check the help of which the nation stands in such sore need?

1909

Woman in the Past and Future

MARGARET McMILLAN

[. . .] *Why* did the militant Suffragette ever come to the door of the House of Commons? How did she ever come into existence at all? And how is it that while thousands of women, more 'intellectual' than she, have asked for the vote for years in the most lady-like and constitutional way, and have got nothing for the pains but admiring politeness? – how is it, I say, that she, the militant Suffragette, can forego the admiration, but wants a Vote, and will, if necessary, fight for it, and – yes, let us admit the truth – DIE for it?

When a woman FORGETS to desire admiration, or fear disgrace, when she looks steadily into the face of all that was erst terrible to her, and is willing to throw her life into the scale, then, though her sister-women cry out against her, and the air shakes with contemptuous laughter, still she must be heard. When the tumult dies down – which is merely an interruption – she will be listened to again. *Why does she want the vote?*

In order to answer this we must put platitudes aside, and face the facts of woman's life as we find them in the working-class community *to-day*. It is of no use to look back a century or two, for then, perhaps, we could not understand. Swift as the mountain storm have been the industrial events which have within the last few decades changed the position and prospects of wage-earning women. If these swift happenings have changed the thoughts of only the more intelligent minority as yet, that is not to be wondered at – still less is it to be taken as a pledge of indifference on the part of the majority in the future. What hundreds see to-day, tens of thousands will see to-morrow.

It is a fashion among pretty writers to say that the Home is woman's true sphere. The pretty phrase is TRUE. Woman's whole mission will probably be found at last to consist in making a great home of the whole habitable planet. But in so far as it applies to the actual conditions of life, and pressing necessities and duties of an increasing multitude of women to-day, the phrase is like an arrow shot by a careless hand into the desert air, and with no destination but to fall perhaps at last into some aching heart. The average wage of wool-combers is about 18s. per week, and factory-workers generally hardly average more than 25s. per week. Every new introduction of machinery displaces labour, and every improvement therefore may be said to cheapen labour – the labour of home-builders. Formerly, that is before the introduction of machinery, the wage-earner knew what to expect, but to-day he cannot know, and his wife shares his anxieties. So she goes out to work herself. In Lancashire 62 per cent. go out to work, in Manchester and Birmingham 63 per cent., and in Stockport and

Dundee the number of outworking women is even greater.

It is clear, however, that all these are not married women. A great many wage-earning women – the majority indeed – are unmarried. School-teachers, journalists, domestic servants, shop-assistants, and a great army of producers in an infinite number of trades – among these are many women who support their parents, and fatherless children or orphaned children. They are out in the world, and are breadwinners, not because they chose to labour in this way, but because the conditions of modern industrial life have compelled them. Woe to them if they hesitate!

I have in my mind the sad case of a noble, *womanly* woman, skilled in all womanly arts, left to struggle alone with her young orphan children. She sewed, she cooked, she kept her home as clean as a jewel; she nursed and tended and taught her little ones. She earned money, too, by taking in washing and going out to cook sometimes, and she died of exhaustion and semi-starvation at last. Her case is not a very uncommon one. A home may be a necessity, but for many it is a luxury. 'She should have gone out to earn and taken a proper situation,' said the victim's brother. It seems a brutal speech, but is it more thoughtlessly cruel than the speech of the fashionable novel-writer who says, 'She should have reigned as queen in her *home*?'

Terrible is the fate of the poor woman who clings to-day to home. The worst paid of all workers are the woman home-workers. It is they who figure in the sweating industries exhibitions, and it is they who dare not ask for justice even in a whisper, and who toil on till wages reach starvation point. Out in the open things are not nearly so bad.

Out in the open women begin to combine, and what is more, they begin to look abroad over the great world of industrial life, and to perceive that its progress consists of ever-growing powers of combination, and that those who take part in its life cannot be long home-workers in the old sense. In short, they begin to see that all unknown to themselves, and almost in spite of themselves, they have to become citizens.

The burdens of citizenship have been assumed by them already. A married woman is responsible for her own acts even to the point of suffering the extreme penalty of the law for certain offences. She is a producer in the industrial markets of the world, a tax and rate payer; and in one constituency at least women trades unionists pay the salary of a representative in Parliament. There is 'a disability to bear arms' – but no disability to go to the help of soldiers, as the numerous corps of army nurses who have served in battle can testify! One by one the burdens of citizenship have been assumed, and because of this fact every thinking wage-earner was bound to get a glimpse of the outer world from which she had been so long excluded. Many begin to look forth at last. And what do they see?

They see, to begin with, that the mediæval notion of home – as a prison for mothers as well as a cradle for children – has little to recommend it. In the stately homes of England there may be room to live, room for romance and idealism. But the number of these homes is small in comparison with the number of one-tenement and two-tenement rooms! In all some 120,000 babes die every year, and not 30 per cent. of all school-going children are thoroughly healthy and well cared for. Bad as all this is, it was infinitely worse in the 'good old days.' 'The grace of hospitality is gone, and the art of good manners.' Perhaps, but the black plague is gone too, and a whole bevy of horrible diseases; drunkenness is declining, and the dreadful things it brings in its train. Little was heard of these in the old days of stately manners, little was heard of child labour, and of miseries that are now searched out and relieved. The thinking, wage-earning woman may see that to-day is dark, but she does not make the mistake of thinking that yesterday was brighter. Just as the condition of the worker in the great warehouse or factory is better than is that of the poor sweated home-worker, so the condition of the child in an elementary school to-day is better than was that of a child in a slum home, or even in a cottage home yesterday, a home where an overworked mother was trying to combine the task of child-minding with cooking, washing, and housemaid's work.

The thinking, wage-earning woman does not wish then to go back, but forward. The State is not a mere *name* to her – an abstraction. Whether she willed or no, she has had to come into a new relation to it. She sees that there is a larger life, and that she has to become an active and conscious part of it. Every year, whether she will or not, this fact is forced home. She may do her duty in the old-world sense well enough, but that will not save her or her dear ones. Of what use to keep her little ones clean and sweet if they have to sit with diseased and neglected children – as they probably must to-day?

The question of wages, of public health, of education, of housing, her fate in sickness, in widowhood, in sudden calamity, in old age – the fate of all the unfortunate, the lost, the suffering, the helpless – all these can not long remain matters of indifference. They are forced daily on her attention in painful and intimate ways. But she can have little or no voice in them, save in co-operation with her fellows: that is to say, she has for larger social purposes little power save as a citizen.

These last words will raise a cry of protest, and bring me face to face with the whole army of the critics of Suffragette methods!

'The clever woman,' says a lady writer, 'sits at home and, like a meadow spider, spreads a pretty web of rose and gold, spangled with diamond dew. Flies – or men – tumble in by scores, and she holds them all prisoners at her pleasure with a silken strand as fine as a hair. But,' she adds, 'her weaving must not be to hold the flies solely for her own amusement – she must learn to use her powers for the betterment of the world.'

The woman making webs, the man tumbling in and being inspired in a trap – is an old, old picture. It was conceived first of all in a warm climate, where unwholesome moisture rose from the teeming earth and made a dimness about the paths of men. It was developed in lands where women, become spinners indeed, were yet confined in close and shadowy chambers, and lost in unwholesome reveries the mere remembrance of the nature and source of inspiration. The very notion of an inspiring spider is alien, however, after all to the average Western – above all to the Saxon. 'I will look up unto the hills from whence cometh my aid,' sang even an Eastern poet, who, we were told, had nevertheless a large harem, and this desire to look not into an intriguing face, however fair, but into the light filled spaces of the Eternal, lives and will live anew in the hearts of our countrymen. This Suffragist – who is accused of having no beauty – will not, at least, prevent them. *She is* not here to make webs, but for other purposes. All the graces of the daughters of slave-women, even when shown forth, as they are to-day in the work of some of our leading women writers, and even their virtues, wholesome enough though a little confined, like flowers in pots, have ceased to awaken her envy. In the storm and stress of workaday life she has been forced to leave such things – to leave them to the women who can cultivate and enjoy them. The rude call of Life summons her elsewhither – and she will not turn back. Perhaps one day – she will find a new charm, a new spell to win love and happiness, but in any case she will not turn back. Just as in the wild forest and its storms the barbarian Northmen conceived a new reverence for women, so in the storm of industrial life, and exposed to all its waves and buffetings, she must learn a new reverence for herself.

1909

'Why I Want the Vote'

MAUD ARNCLIFFE SENNETT

I want the Vote because Lord Curzon says 'it is the imperishable heritage of the human race,' and therefore it belongs to me.

I want it because the young workmen over the age of twenty-one whom I employ are going to the polls to proudly register their Imperial views on the Budget and Tariff Reform, while I, a middle-aged woman, sit in my office and construct the means by which they earn their living, yet am shut out myself.

I want it because I do not see why the women I employ – skilled workers, the chief or sole supporters of their humble homes – should not, the same as men, protect their labour and their other interests at the polls. I want the vote because I pay to educate the children of my older workmen, yet they, who pay no rates or taxes, are marching to the ballot-box, and the Government, which impudently robs me of my hard-earned money, would send me to prison as a third-class criminal were I to walk to St Stephen's [the Houses of Parliament] and importune for a hearing to redress my grievances.

I want the Vote because Mr Lloyd George received a deputation of footballers who, in order to protect their playgrounds, claimed exemption from the land taxes in the proposed Budget; yet deputations of women desperately claiming protection for their livelihood and lives are derided and declined a hearing!

I want it because of the ever-increasing numbers of poor women who are annually murdered in this country, and because of the horrible apathy with which Parliament and Society meet the wholescale destruction of these girls and the hideous system revealed in such cases as the late Brixton one.

I want it because Daisy Lord is being detained for the term of her natural life, while the author of her agony, who abandoned her to her fate, is still at large – a voter, or potential one. I want the authority, which my responsibility as an experienced, thinking, intelligent member of the community demands, to reconstruct the false and cruel standard of morality by which forlorn maternity is so often plunged in the mire, and in its fear and frenzy driven to kill the thing it loves and longs for, namely, its young.

I want it for woman's work – to educate children, house the poor, protect the mother spirit, to vote away the bad divorce law which the 'Englishman's sense of fair play' has thought good enough for English wives! Lady McLaren's Charter would, at one fell stroke, uproot the many wrongs from which our women suffer; but how to force that Charter home without the weapon of the Vote? Impossible! – and that is why I want it!

The Vote, journal of the Women's Freedom League, 1910.

Some Reasons Why Working Women Want the Vote.

1. – Because as long as women cannot vote for Members of Parliament they are not asked what they want, and they are treated like children who do not know what is good or what is bad for them.

2. – Because only those who wear the shoe know where it pinches, and women know best what they want and what they don't want.

3. – Because Members of Parliament must attend to the wants and wishes of those who have votes, and they have not time to attend to the wants and wishes of women who have not got votes.

4. – Because laws are made which specially affect women's work and the work of their children.

5. – Because if women are working as dressmakers, tailoresses, printers, confectioners, and laundresses, or in any factory or workshop, the laws under which they work are made for women without women being asked if these laws are good or bad for them.

6. – Because if the laws under which women work are bad, women cannot have those laws changed unless they have the vote.

7. – Because the vote has been given to women in some of our Colonies and has been of great use.

8. – Because the way to help women is to give them the means of helping themselves.

9. – Because the vote is the best and most direct way by which women can get their wishes and wants attended to.

National Union of Woman's
Suffrage Societies, 1913

Letter to Members of the Women's Social and Political Union

EMMELINE PANKHURST

Dear Friend,

The Prime Minister has announced that in the week beginning January 20th the Women's Amendments to the Manhood Suffrage Bill will be discussed and voted upon. This means that within a few short days the fate of these Amendments will be finally decided.

The W.S.P.U. has from the first declined to call any truce on the strength of the Prime Minister's so-called pledge, and has refused to depend upon the Amendments in question, because the Government have not accepted the responsibility of getting them carried. There are, however, some Suffragists – and there may be some even in the ranks of the W.S.P.U. – who hope against hope that in spite of the Government's intrigues an unofficial Amendment may be carried. Feeling as they do, these Suffragists are tempted to hold their hand as far as militancy is concerned, until after the fate of the Amendments is known.

But every member of the W.S.P.U. recognises that the defeat of the Amendments will make militancy more a moral duty and more a political necessity than it has ever been before. We must prepare beforehand to deal with that situation!

There are degrees of militancy. Some women are able to go further than others in militant action and each woman is the judge of her own duty so far as that is concerned. To be militant in some way or other is, however, a moral obligation. It is a duty which every woman will owe to her own conscience and self-respect, to other women who are less fortunate than she herself is, and to all those who are to come after her.

If any woman refrains from militant protest against the injury done by the Government and the House of Commons to women and to the race, she will share the responsibility for the crime. Submission under such circumstances will be itself a crime.

I know that the defeat of the Amendments will prove to thousands of women that to rely only on peaceful, patient methods, is to court failure, and that militancy is inevitable.

We must, as I have said, prepare to meet the crisis before it arises. Will you therefore tell me (by letter, if it is not possible to do so by word of mouth), that you are ready to take your share in manifesting in a practical manner your indignation at the betrayal of our cause.

Yours sincerely,
(Signed) E. Pankhurst
10 January, 1913

Extract from Special Branch report

ANNIE KENNEY

Miss A. Kenney opened her speech by referring to the Labour Conference, and made an attack on the Labour Party. Continuing she said, 'They have not promised any more than what Mr Balfour promised in 1907. We demand that the Labour Party shall vote against the Government, not on the Franchise Bill alone, but on every question that comes up in the House of Commons, until they have voted them out of Office. This is our campaign: – We have got to turn the Government out. At every street corner and place where we have public meeting we must instil into the minds of the public that unless the Government gives way, and bring in a Bill to enfranchise women, we must make everyone talk of turning the Government out. We have got to have it ringing in the minds of everyone in the country – Turn the Government out! Turn the Government out!!

'What have we to do? We have got to fight on. I should like to see a sandwich board going all over London, and on the top marked, "Wanted some good window smashers". That is what we want. You know that every woman ought never to go out without a hammer in her pocket, and never to go out, at least without touching one pillar box. You, who cannot break windows, for goodness sake get on with something else. Everyone can do a pillar box, for you must remember that that is the one thing that touches the pockets of the people. How do they know their letters are [not] going to be destroyed? They don't know when their pillar box is going to be attacked, therefore, it is the duty of every Suffragist and Suffragette to go on attacking every pillar box throughout the country, and breaking every window they can without being caught. What we have to do is, we have not to say "Oh, only 50 arrests"!, but, "thank goodness only 50 of them caught"!, and here we are thousands of us. Don't let us be too keen on getting arrested, but get off if we can, and do some more damage. It is no good women thinking of other people doing it. It is your duty, every woman in this audience not only to sympathise with militancy, it is your duty to create such a situation, that unless you all take your part in creating that situation, that situation will not be created. Let us all go home to-night, and see what we can do and create a situation. We want to see what is going to happen at the National Art Gallery and Museums. Let us make it like siege. You cannot all do it, but you can do some little thing to make life unbearable. We have got to take it seriously, and we will all play our part. It does not say we will all get caught. I was asked to say this some time ago, but I would not. To-night I will say it. "He who fights and runs away, lives to fight another day". We have got to fight one day and get away to fight another day. Women of our Union, Let [*sic*] us make London absolutely unbearable for the average citizen, until the average citizen along with the shopkeepers will go on a deputation and fill Charing Cross to Palace Yard with people, to tell the Government that women shall have the vote at once. We can easily do it. Come out in numbers. So when you go home to-night think of what scheme you can do, and go and do it; lose no time, but get on with your business. It will have more effect on the men in the street than any public meeting you can hold. We have got to hold meetings, but the only thing you have got to be is militant! militant! and more militant!!!['']

Mrs G. Brackenbury reiterated Mrs Pankhurst's remarks, and asked for volunteers to join the Union, and invited questions, which were answered by Mrs Pankhurst, who in reply to one of the questions said, 'That it was absolutely untrue that the members of the W.S.P.U. had used or intended to use vitriol or revolvers in the course of their campaign.'

A collection was then made, and the meeting which was attended by about 500 women and 20 men terminated 10.p.m., and dispersed quietly.

Essex Hall, The Strand, London, 31 January 1913.

Married Women's Work and Infantile Mortality

SELINA COOPER

MADAM, – The statement made by Mr John Burns at the recent Conference in London on Infantile Mortality that the high death-rate in the cotton towns of Lancashire was due to the employment of married women in the factories, has aroused a great deal of discussion, and as the above statement will be accepted by many as the cause of the high death-rate, it may interest the readers of THE COMMON CAUSE to have a few facts put before them from a working-woman's point of view.

In my letter to the *Manchester Guardian* of the 7th inst., I pointed out the low infantile death-rate of Nelson, where quite as large a percentage of married women work as weavers as in the other Lancashire towns quoted by Mr John Burns with a much higher death-rate. In the recent Medical Officer's Report of Nelson, the infantile death-rate was given as 77.3 per 1,000, nearly the same as Hampstead, mentioned by Mr Burns as a model in this respect, and less than Battersea with 83 per 1,000. Mr Burns implies that Battersea may boast of the low figure, because of the non-existence of married women's labour. Then how does he account for Nelson's still lower figure, where most married women are wage-earners – and its equal rate with Hampstead, which he considers a model rate?

I do not think that the above question will be answered by the President of the Local Government Board. He has made the statement that the loss of child life is due to married women going out to work, and no doubt he will stick to it. But that is not so. alarming as the fact that working women are voteless, and their power to check panic legislation, which may take the form of prohibiting married women from having the right to work without giving her other means whereby she can assert her own individuality is 'very limited indeed.'

The sense of fair play is not always shown when legislators discuss the important question of child life. The very fact that nature has ordained women to be the mothers of the race causes public opinion to turn its criticism towards her first when children are suffering. I once took part in a discussion on married women's labour at a conference. The arguments were based on one particular line of thought. Some pitied the mother, others blamed her; a few suggested certain means of educating the mother on her responsibility towards her children. When I stated that a little attention ought to be given to see that the fathers did their duty, no one had any idea that they needed any attention.

One reason why I am a convinced Suffragist is that the mothers (even as wage-earners) take the greater share of responsibility in the upbringing of their children; therefore, they ought to have the greater means, not less, to enable them to do justice to the rising generation. The mothers of Lancashire are not shirking their duty as parents any more than working-women of other counties; the truth is that they are falling into line with the changed economic conditions, which demand a higher standard of life, and to supply the means of the higher cost of living, along with the growing desire to partake of some of the pleasures of life, they have with their characteristic grit, turned out to work, to earn money to meet the new conditions. According to Mr John Burns's figures, they have been the means of placing Lancashire in the lowest scale of pauperism in this country. The working women of Lancashire do not claim that they are endowed with superhuman abilities, alone to resist the forces which are tending towards the deterioration of the race; but what they do claim is, that they are human beings, struggling hard to develop their own economic independence: therefore preparing for the time when men and women will face the great problem of the loss of child life in the councils of the nation. – Yours, &c.,

SELINA COOPER
The Common Cause, 22 August 1913.

Princess's Unpaid Taxes

FINES UPON FOUR SUMMONSES

The Princess Sophia Duleep Singh, residing at Hampton-road, Hampton Court, attended at Feltham Police Court yesterday upon summonses for refusing to pay taxes. She employed a groom without a licence, and also kept two dogs and a carriage without paying for the necessary licences. She came to court wearing the badge and medal of the Tax Resistance League and was accompanied by six other ladies, including the secretary of the league, Mrs Kineton Parkes.

After evidence had been given by an officer of Inland Revenue, the princess read a statement which she had written with pencil on a sheet of foolscap. It contained this passage:

'When the women of England are enfranchised and the State acknowledges me as a citizen I shall, of course, pay my share willingly to its upkeep.'

The chairman (Mr J. Ashby) said the Bench had nothing to do with all that.

Mr White (supervisor of taxes) said the princess was convicted of a similar offence in May 1911.

Fines were imposed on the four summonses, amounting to £12 10s., with costs.

The princess said she wished it clearly understood that she would not pay these taxes, and, she added, 'I don't say I will pay these fines, either.'

Daily Mail, 13 December 1913

Freedom or Death

EMMELINE PANKHURST

SPEECH DELIVERED AT HARTFORD, CONNECTICUT

I do not come here as an advocate, because whatever position the suffrage movement may occupy in the United States of America, in England it has passed beyond the realm of advocacy and it has entered into the sphere of practical politics. It has become the subject of revolution and civil war, and so tonight I am not here to advocate woman suffrage. American suffragists can do that very well for themselves.

I am here as a soldier who has temporarily left the field of battle in order to explain – it seems strange it should have to be explained – what civil war is like when civil war is waged by women. I am not only here as a soldier temporarily absent from the field at battle; I am here – and that, I think, is the strangest part of my coming – I am here as a person who, according to the law courts of my country, it has been decided, is of no value to the community at all; and I am adjudged because of my life to be a dangerous person, under sentence of penal servitude in a convict prison.

It is not at all difficult if revolutionaries come to you from Russia, if they come to you from China, or from any other part of the world, if they are men. But since I am a woman it is necessary to explain why women have adopted revolutionary methods in order to win the rights of citizenship. We women, in trying to make our case clear, always have to make as part of our argument, and urge upon men in our audience the fact – a very simple fact – that women are human beings.

Suppose the men of Hartford had a grievance, and they laid that grievance before their legislature, and the legislature obstinately refused to listen to them, or to remove their grievance, what would be the proper and the constitutional and the practical way of getting their grievance removed? Well, it is perfectly obvious at the next general election the men of Hartford would turn out that legislature and elect a new one.

But let the men of Hartford imagine that they were not in the position of being voters at all, that they were governed without their consent being obtained, that the legislature turned an absolutely deaf ear to their demands, what would the men of Hartford do then? They couldn't vote the legislature out. They would have to choose; they would have to make a choice of two evils: they would either have to submit indefinitely to an unjust state of affairs, or they would have to rise up and adopt some of the antiquated means by which men in the past got their grievances remedied.

Your forefathers decided that they must have representation for taxation, many, many years ago. When they felt they couldn't wait any longer, when they laid all the arguments before an obstinate British government that they could think of, and when their arguments were absolutely disregarded, when every other means had failed, they began by the tea party at Boston, and they went on until they had won the independence of the United States of America.

It is about eight years since the word militant was first used to describe what we were doing. It was not militant at all, except that it provoked militancy on the part of those who were opposed to it. When women asked questions in political meetings and failed to get answers, they were not doing anything militant. In Great Britain it is a custom, a time-honoured one, to ask questions of candidates for parliament and ask questions of members of the government. No man was ever put out of a public meeting for asking a question. The first people who were put out of a political meeting for asking questions, were women; they were brutally ill-used; they found themselves in jail before 24 hours had expired.

We were called militant, and we were quite willing to accept the name. We were determined to press this question of the enfranchisement of women to the point where we were no longer to be ignored by the politicians.

You have two babies very hungry and wanting to be fed. One baby is a patient baby, and waits indefinitely until its mother is ready to feed it.

The other baby is an impatient baby and cries lustily, screams and kicks and makes everybody unpleasant until it is fed. Well, we know perfectly well which baby is attended to first. That is the whole history of politics. You have to make more noise than anybody else, you have to make yourself more obtrusive than anybody else, you have to fill all the papers more than anybody else, in fact you have to be there all the time and see that they do not snow you under.

When you have warfare things happen; people suffer; the noncombatants suffer as well as the combatants. And so it happens in civil war. When your forefathers threw the tea into Boston Harbour, a good many women had to go without their tea. It has always seemed to me an extraordinary thing that you did not follow it up by throwing the whiskey overboard; you sacrificed the women; and there is a good deal of warfare for which men take a great deal of glorification which has involved more practical sacrifice on women than it has on any man. It always has been so. The grievances of those who have got power, the influence of those who have got power commands a great deal of attention; but the wrongs and the grievances of those people who have no power at all are apt to be absolutely ignored. That is the history of humanity right from the beginning.

Well, in our civil war people have suffered, but you cannot make omelettes without breaking eggs; you cannot have civil war without damage to something. The great thing is to see that no more damage is done than is absolutely necessary, that you do just as much as will arouse enough feeling to bring about peace, to bring about an honourable peace for the combatants; and that is what we have been doing.

We entirely prevented stockbrokers in London from telegraphing to stockbrokers in Glasgow and vice versa: for one whole day telegraphic communication was entirely stopped. I am not going to tell you how it was done. I am not going to tell you how the women got to the mains and cut the wires; but it was done.

It was done, and it was proved to the authorities that weak women, suffrage women, as we are supposed to be, had enough ingenuity to create a situation of that kind. Now, I ask you, if women can do that, is there any limit to what we can do except the limit we put upon ourselves?

If you are dealing with an industrial revolution, if you get the men and women of one class rising up against the men and women of another class, you can locate the difficulty; if there is a great industrial strike, you know exactly where the violence is and how the warfare is going to be waged; but in our war against the government you can't locate it. We wear no mark; we belong to every class; we permeate every class of the community from the highest to the lowest; and so you see in the woman's civil war the dear men of my country are discovering it is absolutely impossible to deal with it: you cannot locate it, and you cannot stop it.

'Put them in prison,' they said, 'that will stop it.' But it didn't stop it at all: instead of the women giving it up, more women did it, and more and more and more women did it until there were 300 women at a time, who had not broken a single law, only 'made a nuisance of themselves' as the politicians say.

Then they began to legislate. The British government has passed more stringent laws to deal with this agitation than it ever found necessary during all the history of political agitation in my country. They were able to deal with the revolutionaries of the Chartists' time; they were able to deal with the trades union agitation; they were able to deal with the revolutionaries later on when the Reform Acts were passed: but the ordinary law has not sufficed to curb insurgent women. They had to dip back into the middle ages to find a means of repressing the women in revolt.

They have said to us, government rests upon force, the women haven't force, so they must submit.

Well, we are showing them that government does not rest upon force at all: it rests upon consent. As long as women consent to be unjustly governed, they can be, but directly women say: 'We withhold our consent, we will not be governed any longer so long as that government is unjust.' Not by the forces of civil war can you govern the very weakest woman. You can kill that woman, but she escapes you then; you cannot govern her. No power on earth can govern a human being, however feeble, who withholds his or her consent.

When they put us in prison at first, simply for taking

petitions, we submitted; we allowed them to dress us in prison clothes; we allowed them to put us in solitary confinement; we allowed them to put us amongst the most degraded of criminals; we learned of some of the appalling evils of our so-called civilisation that we could not have learned in any other way. It was valuable experience, and we were glad to get it.

I have seen men smile when they heard the words 'hunger strike', and yet I think there are very few men today who would be prepared to adopt a 'hunger strike' for any cause. It is only people who feel an intolerable sense of oppression who would adopt a means of that kind. It means you refuse food until you are at death's door, and then the authorities have to choose between letting you die, and letting you go; and then they let the women go.

Now, that went on so long that the government felt that they were unable to cope. It was [then] that, to the shame of the British government, they set the example to authorities all over the world of feeding sane, resisting human beings by force. There may be doctors in this meeting: if so, they know it is one thing to feed by force an insane person; but it is quite another thing to feed a sane, resisting human being who resists with every nerve and with every fibre of her body the indignity and the outrage of forcible feeding.

Now, that was done in England, and the government thought they had crushed us. But they found that it did not quell the agitation, that more and more women came in and even passed that terrible ordeal, and they were obliged to let them go.

Then came the legislation – the 'Cat and Mouse Act'. The home secretary said: 'Give me the power to let these women go when they are at death's door, and leave them at liberty under license until they have recovered their health again and then bring them back.' It was passed to repress the agitation, to make the women yield – because that is what it has really come to, ladies and gentlemen. It has come to a battle between the women and the government as to who shall yield first, whether they will yield and give us the vote, or whether we will give up our agitation.

Well, they little know what women are. Women are very slow to rouse, but once they are aroused, once they are determined, nothing on earth and nothing in heaven will make women give way; it is impossible. And so this 'Cat and Mouse Act' which is being used against women today has failed. There are women lying at death's door, recovering enough strength to undergo operations who have not given in and won't give in, and who will be prepared, as soon as they get up from their sick beds, to go on as before. There are women who are being carried from their sick beds on stretchers into meetings. They are too weak to speak, but they go amongst their fellow workers just to show that their spirits are unquenched, and that their spirit is alive, and they mean to go on as long as life lasts.

Now, I want to say to you who think women cannot succeed, we have brought the government of England to this position, that it has to face this alternative: either women are to be killed or women are to have the vote.

I ask American men in this meeting, what would you say if in your state you were faced with that alternative, that you must either kill them or give them their citizenship? Well, there is only one answer to that alternative, there is only one way out – you must give those women the vote.

You won your freedom in America when you had the revolution, by bloodshed, by sacrificing human life. You won the civil war by the sacrifice of human life when you decided to emancipate the negro. You have left it to women in your land, the men of all civilised countries have left it to women, to work out their own salvation. That is the way in which we women of England are doing. Human life for us is sacred, but we say if any life is to be sacrificed it shall be ours; we won't do it ourselves, but we will put the enemy in the position where they will have to choose between giving us freedom or giving us death.

So here am I. I come in the intervals of prison appearance. I come after having been four times imprisoned under the 'Cat and Mouse Act', probably going back to be rearrested as soon as I set my foot on British soil. I come to ask you to help to win this fight. If we win it, this hardest of all fights, then, to be sure, in the future it is going to be made easier for women all over the world to win their fight when their time comes.

13 November, 1913

The Woman's Dreadnought

SYLVIA PANKHURST

Early in 1914 the East London Federation of the W.S.P.U.
changed its name and became the East London Federation of the Suffragettes. We made this change at the
request of others. Our policy remains what it has always
been. We are still a Militant non-party organisation of
working-women.

Some people tell us that it is neither specially important that working-women should agitate for the Vote,
nor specially important that they should have it. They
forget that, comparatively, the leisured, comfortably
situated women are but a little group, and the working-
women a multitude.

Some people say that the lives of working-women are
too hard and their education too small for them to
become a powerful force in winning the Vote, many
though they are. Such people have forgotten their history. What sort of women were those who marched to
Versailles?

Those Suffragists who say that it is the duty of the
richer and more fortunate women to win the Vote, and
that their poorer sisters need not feel themselves called

upon to aid in the struggle, appear, in using such arguments, to forget that it is *the Vote* for which we are fighting. The essential principle of the vote is that each one of us shall have a share of power to help himself or herself and us all. It is in direct opposition to the idea that some few, who are more favoured, shall help and teach and patronize the others. It is surely because we Suffragists believe in the principle that every individual and every class of individuals has a right to a share both in ruling and in serving, and because we have learnt by long and bitter experience that every form of government but self-government is tyranny – however kindly its intention – that we are fighting for the Vote, and not for the remedying of some of the many particular grievances from which women suffer.

It is necessary for women to fight for the Vote because, by means of the Vote, if we combine in sufficient numbers to use it for definite ends, we can win reforms for ourselves by making it plain to Governments that they must either give us the things we want, or make way for those that will. Working-women – sweated women, wage slaves, overworked mothers toiling in little homes – these, of all created beings, stand in the greatest need of this, the power to help themselves.

One of the principle reasons why it is essential that working-women should rise up in a body and work strenuously for the Vote is that when the Franchise Question at last comes up for actual settlement, the anti-Suffragists in Parliament will struggle to reduce the number of women voters as far as possible. Any restrictions that they may seek to impose are practically certain to operate most hardly against the poorest women, and the only thing that can safeguard their position is a big and active working-women's Franchise Agitation.

The Reformers of old *worked* to extend the boundaries of human freedom, because they believed the principle to be right, but they *fought and suffered and strove with desperate courage*, because they were spurred on by the knowledge that they or their fellows were suffering and in need. So it is to-day with those who want the Vote.

We have a tremendous task before us. We are only fighting with the courage with which men fight, the Government, and men in the mass, will only see the suffering and the fighting of the men. Only when we bear infinitely more than men, and struggle infinitely harder, will men care enough or understand enough to help women to be politically free. So we must go on striving, and try always to see the greatness of our aim.

Extract from *The Woman's Dreadnought*, 8 March 1914

The Price of Liberty

EMILY WILDING DAVISON

The true suffragette is an epitome of the determination of women to possess their own souls. The words of the Master are eternally true:

> 'What shall it profit a man if he gain the whole world and lose his own soul?'

And it is the realisation of this ideal that is moving the most advanced of the feminists to stand out at all costs to-day.

Men, as a sex, have not yet grasped the inevitability of the forging of this last link in the chain of human progress. Ever since history peeps out of the mists of time, the male of the race has made it his prerogative to give or deny the whole world to his partner, but has withheld from her that which is above all temporal things, namely, the possession of a soul, the manifestation of the Godhead within.

FORGETTING THE MIGHTY SPIRIT

They have beautified and decorated the shrine, but they have kept it empty of the divinity which gave a significance to the paraphernalia of the shrine.

Especially is this error noticeable and blameworthy in the latter days of the early Christian Church, when it was seriously discussed whether women even possessed souls, and sufficient doubt on the subject was raised to condemn the sex from that time onward to an inferior position in the community.

For centuries people have been groping after the dry bones of humanity, forgetting the mighty spirit which alone could make those dry bones live, till early last century the sons of men saw the need of the vivifying breath, and one man after another, one class after another, felt the quick, stirring process, and rose to the wonderous life of civic freedom.

Could the partners of men be untouched by this marvellous awakening? Could women any longer remain dry bones merely, or indeed even as a clod of earth in the valley? Could the newly-aroused and enlightened race owe its origin to an insensate and unintelligent creature?

THE PARABLE OF MILITANCY

The wonderful Renascence of Freedom has to extend its kindly influence to all! In the New Testament the

Master reminded His followers that when the merchant had found the Pearl of Great Price, he sold all that he had in order to buy it. That is the parable of Militancy! It is that which the women warriors are doing to-day.

Some are truer warriors than others, but the perfect Amazon is she who will sacrifice all even unto this last, to win the Pearl of Freedom for her sex.

Some of the beauteous pearls that women sell to obtain this freedom which is so little appreciated by those who are born free are the pearls of Friendship, Good Report, Love, and even Life itself, each in itself a priceless boon.

Who will gainsay that Friendship is one of the priceless jewels of life? Did not the Elizabeth philosopher remind us that Friendship doubles our joys and halves our sorrows? Have not the poets sung the inestimable riches of Friendship?

Yet this pearl is sacrificed without a moment's hesitation by the true militant. And, indeed, the sacrifice is inevitable, even as the sun puts out the bright glow of the grate fire. Yet the Lares and Penates are valued gods, even if lesser lights, whilst on the sunniest day a bitter frost may necessitate the worship of the lesser but more comfortable flame.

Thus the sacrifice involves terrible suffering to the militant, – old friends, recently-made friends, they all go, one by one, into the limbo of the burning, fiery furnace – a grim holocaust to Liberty.

An even severer part of the price is the surrender of Good Report, one of the brightest and most precious of the gems in a woman's crown, as anyone can realise who knows how easily her fair fame is sullied.

Men have been able to go forward through good report and ill report, and so low has been the standard of morals for them that the breath of scandal but seemed to burnish more brightly their good qualities.

But owing to the same double standard the merest whisper of venomous tongues could damn a woman socially and politically, for to be safe she must be like Cæsar's wife.

Hence, to women, reputation is often as dear as life itself. Yet even this jewel has been sacrificed by the militant, for she felt the truth of the Cavalier poet's song –

'I could not love thee, dear, so much,
Loved I not honour more.'

And she has felt in her innermost soul that there was no chance of preserving any 'honour' worth the name if she acquiesced in a state of society wherein women's souls and bodies were bought and sold.

'Ye cannot serve God and Mammon.' What possibility for those who knew the existing evil to sit down and suffer it in comfort and peace? Better to be Anathema Maranatha for the sake of progress than to sit lapped in ignoble ease in the House of Good Fame! Better that all men should speak evil of her and revile her, fighting the eternal battle of glorious Liberty and Humanity!

But a more soul-rending sacrifice even than that of friendship and of good report is demanded of the Militant – that of the blood-tie. 'She that loveth mother or father, sister or brother, husband or child, dearer than me cannot be my disciple,' saith the terrible voice of Freedom, in accents that rend the very heart in twain.

'EVEN UNTO THIS PRICE'

'Cannot this cup of anguish be spared me,' cries the militant aloud in agony, yet immediately, as if in repentance for having so nearly lost the Priceless Pearl, in the words of all strivers after progress, she ejaculates: 'Nevertheless I will pay, even unto this price,' and in her writhing asks what further demand can be exacted from her.

The glorious and inscrutable Spirit of Liberty has but one further penalty within its power, the surrender of Life itself. It is the supreme consummation of sacrifice, than which none can be higher or greater.

To lay down life for friends, that is glorious, selfless, inspiring! But to re-enact the tragedy of Calvary for generations yet unborn, that is the last consummate sacrifice of the Militant!

'Nor will she shrink from this Nirvana
She will be faithful "unto this last."'

The Suffragette, 5 June 1914. Reprinted from the *Daily Sketch*, 28 May 1914. The article was published posthumously.

The Women's Victory – and After

MILLICENT GARRETT FAWCETT

'In the United States the grant of women's suffrage has made no difference whatever . . . the mere fact that women have a right to vote makes no difference at all.' – VISCOUNT BRYCE, *in House of Lords, December 17th, 1917.*

The words quoted above come strangely from the lips of any man who believes in the principles of free representative government. If the vote makes no difference, why have our race all over the world attached such enormous importance to it? It is bred in our bone, and will never come out of the flesh, that the possession of the franchise is the very foundation-stone of political freedom. Our fifty years' struggle for the women's vote was not actuated by our setting any extraordinary value on the mere power of making a mark on a voting paper once in every three or four years. We did not, except as a symbol of free citizenship, value it as a thing good in itself; we valued it, not as a ribbon to stick in our coat, but for the sake of the equal laws, the enlarged opportunities, the improved status for women which we knew it involved. We worked for it with ardour and passion because it was stuff of the conscience with us that it would benefit not women only, but the whole community; this is what we meant when we called our paper the *Common Cause*. It was the cause of men, women, and children. We believe that men cannot be truly free so long as women are held in political subjection.

We have at present – November, 1919 – only a very short experience of the actual results of women's suffrage. It is less than two years since the parliamentary battle was won, and less than one year since women voted for the first time, but already the practical results of women's suffrage have surpassed our expectations. It is no exaggeration to say that those most closely in touch with work in Parliament on subjects affecting the welfare and status of women were conscious of a change in the atmosphere of the House immediately after the passing of the Reform Bill of 1918. [. . .]

As soon as might be after the Royal Assent had been given to the Reform Bill in February, 1918, the various suffrage societies held their several council meetings to discuss their future action. Some societies dissolved and formed themselves into women citizens' associations. But many resolved to go on working for objects closely allied with their original purpose. The N.U.W.S.S., meeting in council in March, 1918, by a practically unanimous vote resolved to extend its 'objects,' including in the new programme what had formerly been its sole object – 'to obtain the parliamentary franchise for women on the same terms as it is or may be granted to men'; but adding to this two more objects – namely, 'to obtain all other such reforms, economic, legislative, and social, as are necessary to secure a real equality of liberties, status, and opportunities between men and women'; and 'to assist women to realize their responsibility as voters.' The last of these was an indication of the sympathy of the N.U.W.S.S. with the women citizens' associations which were quickly springing into existence.

We should have acted more logically if at the same time that we enlarged our objects we had also adopted a corresponding change in our name. However, on this matter being put to the vote, the old name was retained by a large majority. Many of our members regarded our name as soldiers regard their flag or regimental badge, and were, from motives of sentiment, averse to giving it up.

However, a year's experience proved that it would be really useful and tend to prevent misunderstandings if we changed our name in accordance with the extension of our objects. Therefore, by formal vote of the council in 1919, [. . .] the N.U.W.S.S. ceased to bear its old name and became the National Union of Societies for Equal Citizenship. We hope that the letters N.U.S.E.C. will soon become as well known and be as much beloved by its members as the N.U.W.S.S.

At this same council meeting of 1919 changes were adopted in our method of attacking what had now become our principal work – viz., the achievement of a real equality of status, liberties, and opportunities between men and women. We had learned in the last twelve months that the field thus covered was so vast that success was jeopardized if we scattered our energies over the whole of it. We therefore resolved henceforth at our annual council meetings to select a limited number of subjects deemed ripe for immediate action, and to concentrate on these, so far as practical work was concerned. The first selection for the year 1919–1920 was thus indicated:

1. We demand *equal pay for equal work*. And we demand an open field for women in industrial and professional work.
2. We demand the immediate reform of the *divorce law* and the laws dealing with solicitation and prostitution. An *equal moral standard* must be established.
3. The Government is in favour of *widows' pensions* in principle. By constant pressure we mean to make the House of Commons turn principle into practice. We demand *pensions for civilian widows*.
4. Women must speak for themselves as well as vote. We want to extend the *women's franchise*, and we are determined that *women candidates* holding our equality programme shall be returned to Parliament at the next election.
5. At present women are not legally recognized as the guardians of their children. We are working to secure *equal rights of guardianship* for both parents.

6. Lastly, we are demanding the *opening of the legal
   professions to women*. We wish to enable women
   to become *solicitors, barristers, and magistrates*.

The walls of our Jericho have not fallen at the first
blast of our trumpet, but we have made great progress
in promoting the principle of equal pay for equal work,
and with the familiarizing of the British public with
women as candidates for Parliament. Since the General
Election two or three women have been candidates, and
one, Lady Astor, has been returned by an immense
majority. [. . .]

Suffragists are not labouring under the impression
that because women now have votes no further reform
is needed in our representative system. A large proportion of suffragists are probably in favour of proportional
representation, and would favour its adoption mainly
on the ground that it would secure a much fairer reflection of the whole nation than the present system, which
may, and frequently does, result in the practical exclusion from representation of large masses of the voters.
A good deal of education and spade work in spreading
the principles of proportional representation are necessary on this and other important reforms, but now that
women form a very considerable portion of the elector-
ate they have at least the satisfaction of knowing that
their views on this and other important political issues
count for something, and are actually studied and considered, so that things work out much more rapidly than
ever before in the direction they desire.

The enfranchisement of women, especially the immense addition to the women municipal electors, has put the position of women in local elections on quite a new footing. Formerly, when there were only about a million women voters on the municipal registers of the three kingdoms, and these, in considerable numbers, were either aged or on the brink of old age, they were a negligible quantity. They were neither admitted to the men's organizations nor consulted by them; the candidature of women for locally elected councils was cold-shouldered or opposed by all the party organizations; but the situation is quite different now. The women local electors have increased from one million to eight and a half millions, and, besides this, women are also parliamentary electors; the result is that all the parties encourage the candidature of women, and are pleased to have one or more women's names on their own tickets. Thus the number of women elected in the recent borough council elections in London bounded up on November 1st, 1919, to nearly two hundred. Chelsea, which never returned a woman before, now returns ten; Westminster returns seven; Marylebone returns four, and so on; and the results in many of the country towns were equally remarkable. (See the *Common Cause*, November 7th, 1919.)

Some time ago, in one of my controversies with Mrs Humphry Ward, she lamented the very small number of women offering themselves as candidates in local government elections. I pointed out that the qualification for candidature was such as to exclude, in a large degree, the mass of the younger and more vigorous women; also, that the small number of women holding the local government franchise, coupled with the fact that they had no parliamentary vote, rendered them negligible from the party point of view, and I suggested to Mrs Ward that the best way of increasing the number and improving the status of women concerned in local government would be to secure the abolition of their political disabilities. Events since February, 1918, have more than justified my argument.

Besides the positive gains to women and to the whole country which women's suffrage has brought about, it is satisfactory to note that none of the disasters so freely prophesied by the antisuffragists have materialized. The prophets themselves seem to recognize that they were the baseless fabric of a vision now utterly vanished even from remembrance.

Extract from Millicent Garrett Fawcett, *The Women's Victory – and After: Personal Reminiscences, 1911–1918*

Suffragette Biographies

Barbara Bodichon (1827–1891) was an artist and campaigner. She fought for key pieces of legislation which improved women's rights to divorce and property, and helped to expand women's access to education by founding a school and co-founding Newnham, the women's college. Bodichon formed the first Women's Suffrage Committee, whose petition was presented to the House of Commons by John Stuart Mill.

Frances Power Cobbe (1822–1904) was an Irish writer. She was the author of many books, essays and articles on women's suffrage, property rights and women's access to education. Cobbe also campaigned for animal rights, and helped to legislate against experiments on animals.

Christabel Pankhurst (1880–1958) was the eldest of Emmeline Pankhurst's five children. She had a first class law degree, but was barred from practising as a woman. She helped to found the Women's Social and Political Union (WSPU), and worked as its chief organizer; in this capacity, she was imprisoned on multiple occasions.

Emmeline Pankhurst (1858–1928) was arguably the most famous suffragette. Born in Manchester, she was a founding member of the Women's Franchise League, and led the Women's Social and Political Union. She was a proponent of radical tactics, and was repeatedly imprisoned.

Annie Kenney (1879–1953) began work in a Lancashire textile mill aged ten, while still attending school. Whilst there, she became involved in trade union organizing. After hearing Teresa Billington-Greig and Christabel Pankhurst speak in Oldham in 1905, she became a committed suffragette, was imprisoned several times and ultimately became deputy leader of the WSPU.

Flora Drummond (1878–1949) grew up on the Isle of Arran, and moved to Glasgow aged fourteen. She qualified as a postmistress, but was unable to follow this career because she did not meet the height restriction, and took a secretarial course instead. Drummond later moved to Manchester with her husband, and became an organizer with the WSPU, spending several periods in prison. She was known as the General, because of her habit of riding at the front of processions wearing military regalia.

Eva Gore-Booth (1870–1926) was born into an aristocratic Irish family. She was inspired to join the suffrage struggle after meeting suffragist and social justice campaigner Esther Roper, who became her partner.

Gore-Booth was also involved in adult education for women and trade union activism, and rallying working-class women to the suffrage cause. Outside of activism, she was also a published poet.

Constance Smedley (1876–1941) was born in Birmingham, and was active in the Arts and Crafts movement there. A writer, playwright and artist, she founded the International Association of Lyceum Clubs, as an alternative to gentlemen's clubs, where women could meet outside of the home and get career advice.

Margaret McMillan (1860–1931) was born in New York State, but grew up in Inverness. After working as a governess, she dedicated herself to the cause of child development, nutrition and hygiene. An advocate of progressive nursery education, McMillan founded her own open-air nursery in Deptford, and successfully campaigned for free school meals. She was injured while protesting against the treatment of WSPU prisoners.

Maud Arncliffe Sennett (1862–1936) was born in London; her parents ran a Christmas cracker and confectionary factory. After a successful career as an actress under the stage name Mary Kingsley, she and her husband took over the management of the factory. Sennett campaigned with both the suffragists, as a member of the Women's Freedom League, and the more militant WSPU. At one point, she was imprisoned for breaking the windows of the *Daily Mail* offices.

Selina Cooper (1864–1946) left school at thirteen to work at her local cotton mill in Barnoldswick, Lancashire. Cooper became involved with a trade union, the Burnley Weavers' Association, before joining the North of England Society for Women's Suffrage. A pacifist socialist, she worked as an organizer for both the National Union of Women's Suffrage Societies (NUWSS) and the Independent Labour Party. After settling in Nelson, Lancashire, she established the first maternity centre there, and served as a local magistrate.

Sophia Duleep Singh (1876–1948) was the daughter of the exiled Maharaja of the Sikh Empire, and the goddaughter of Queen Victoria, who gave her an apartment in Hampton Court. She was a leading member of both the WSPU and the Women's Tax Resistance League. Singh was the most prominent woman of Indian heritage in the British suffragette movement, but others were also involved, such as Lolita Roy, Bhagwati Bhola Nauth and Sushama Sen. Their struggle for suffrage also intersected with broader anticolonial movements.

Sylvia Pankhurst (1882–1960) was the second of the five Pankhurst children. She was an artist, who won scholarships to study at Manchester Art School and the Royal College of Art, but chose to focus on the suffrage campaign and socialist politics. She founded and led the East London Federation of Suffragettes (ELFS), after the group was expelled from the WSPU. Alongside its political lobbying, the ELFS served the East End community by setting up canteens, social centres, a cooperative toy factory, a crèche and a nursery. Unlike other suffrage organizations, it continued to campaign throughout the First World War.

Emily Wilding Davison (1872–1913) was born in London. She achieved first-class honours in English, although as a woman she was unable to graduate, and was employed as a teacher before working for the WSPU. Davison spent several periods in prison, where she suffered solitary confinement and force feeding. She died as a result of a suffragette protest, after running out in front of the king's horse at the Epsom Derby in 1913. It is not clear whether she intended to commit suicide.

Millicent Garrett Fawcett (1847–1929) was one of the longest-serving leaders of the suffragist movement. She spoke at the first public meeting at the National Society for Women's Suffrage, in 1869. Later, Garrett Fawcett was President of the NUWSS from 1907 to 1919, and always advocated gradualist, constitutional methods. Alongside her suffrage work she wrote articles, novels, biographies and textbooks, and campaigned for a variety of Liberal political causes.